microwave
FOR CERTAIN

BY
JAMES GARROD
AND **ANNEMARIE ROSIER**

All illustrations by Rupert Besley

WAVEGUIDE
TRAINING AND
PUBLICATIONS

Published by
Waveguide
33 Carter Street
Sandown
Isle of Wight

© Copyright James Garrod
and Annemarie Rosier 1990

ISBN 1 873373 00 7

All rights reserved. No part of this publication may be reproduced, stored in a retrieval system or transmitted in any form or by any means, electronic, electrical, chemical, mechanical, optical, photocopy, recording or otherwise without prior written permission from the publisher to whom all enquiries must be addressed.

Printed by:
Crossprint Limited, Newport, Isle of Wight.

The Sistine Microwave by Michelangelo.

DEDICATION

I dedicate this book to Timothy Smidger, the ginger cat who spent many long hours with me at the word processor during its creation. His incessant purring helped enormously in bringing the information and ideas into print.   J G

Contents

Page

12	Your Views Reviewed
14	What the Oven Is
16	Wattages
19	What the Oven Does
21	How You Should Help It
22	Getting the Food Right
24	Timing Pros and Cons
25	Dispensing with Timings
26	[CU] The key to success
27	The New Procedures Introduced
29	What Variable Power Is
30	What Variable Power Does
33	De-frosting
35	More Efficient De-frosting
36	Perfect De-frosting
37	Perfect Re-heating
39	Christmas Food Problems
40	Cookware and Browning Dish
41	Probes, Thermometers and Sensors
42	Combination Ovens
45	Foods and Recipes
51	Breakfast food
51	Vegetables
54	Fruit
56	Fish
58	Pasta and Rice
61	Poultry
63	Sauces
65	Scrambled eggs
65	Meat
68	Puddings
72	Cakes and Bakes
74	Menu Planning
75	Looking after Your Oven
83	The Small Print
87	What Went Wrong

PREFACE

This book had to be written in simple terms for everyone to understand, and at the same time it had to be technically correct. I am glad I was asked to read the manuscript to confirm that it was so, for it was a pleasant surprise to find such extensive information, and I found myself reading it over and over again. It is indeed scientifically sound.

To cater for those who are technically inclined, The Small Print explains things in greater detail and reveals some very interesting facts. It will make good supplementary training for anyone connected with microwave oven sales or servicing. In fact, the same can be said of the book as a whole.

As a major manufacturer of microwave ovens, GoldStar know how important it is for these appliances to be used intelligently. Some people quickly take to microwave, whilst others have difficulty breaking away from the familiar heat and temperatures. The microwave story as told in this book should leave no cause for doubt or confusion, and it may be an eye-opener even to the most successful microwave cook.

I particularly like the chapter on how to look after a microwave oven and recognise whether or not it needs attention. I think this is the first publication to offer comprehensive advice along those lines. I know for sure that engineers are often called out to microwave ovens which are in no way faulty.

Everyone who uses a microwave oven has something to gain by reading this book, especially if they follow it through right from the beginning. I strongly recommend they do just that.

Paul Martindale

Senior Technical and Service Manager
GoldStar (UK) Ltd.

GoldStar, a leading electronics manufacturer in Korea, now have operations in over eighty countries worldwide. They design and manufacture microwave ovens which appear in the U.K. under various well known brand names.

Introduction

Some people succeed with a microwave oven while others fail, even when they all work strictly according to the book. The reasons for this are various, but they usually have one thing in common - they affect the timings laid down for general use. For example, food temperature and moisture content will vary from one home to the next, and even at the same place on different occasions. We call such things "uncertainties", and they are listed on page 10. It is quite impossible to alter timings to make up for so many things.

Now we reveal to everyone that there are superior methods which do not use timings. They are not altogether new, even though they are almost unknown to the general public. By adopting them, you'll be using microwave with certainty.

There's a bonus. These simple procedures can also provide you with your own, individual, tried and tested timings

A common problem is that microwave is easily confused with the conventional. For example, power levels are often thought to be like temperatures. In fact, they are very different.

When microwave ovens first came into the shops, simplified instructions were essential. That is when the idea of timings became established. It also meant adapting conventional procedures which were not altogether compatible with microwave. They are still around, outliving their usefulness.

Here, we present true microwave methods and ideas. They are a perfect grounding for the new generation of microwave user, and a godsend to anyone who is less than entirely successful with a microwave oven. They offer the best chance of success first time. Curiously, our great grandmothers must have used similar procedures with their stoves, so they are in no way high-tech.

Compared with the risky "set it and forget it" system, these methods do need more attention, but it's a small price to pay for perfection.

A great relief is that we have no use for any mumbo jumbo such as friction of molecules. Your main concern is what happens to the food and drink, and you'll know exactly what to expect, once you understand your oven and how it behaves. That's why your first step is to get to know it better.

Clearly, we shall frown on using the microwave oven as though it were a video recorder. Setting it up from a list of times, and taking a chance on the outcome. That's not for us.

Many microwave cookbooks contain good basic information, and you're bound to have at least one such book, so use it in conjunction with this one. We repeat and sometimes clarify the points which are most important to our procedures.

Your plan for success is this. Avoid making the common mistake of starting with the recipes, and READ THE BOOK THROUGH IN ITS WRITTEN SEQUENCE. It has been painstakingly assembled with the sole aim of making you really good with your microwave oven, and you cannot improve on it by reading only the parts you fancy. Enjoy whatever appeals to you most, but do make sure you read everything else. We've put together a balanced diet which any serious microwave user can digest. It is not padded out with useless stodge.

All the usual foods are included, and throughout, the emphasis is on getting things right. That's desirable at any time, but vital with defrosting and re-heating.

The food chapters are in harmony with the new methods. The first recipe in each group demonstrates the relevant procedure, and blends it with well proved microwave cookery techniques. The things you have read about will be happening right before your eyes, and entirely under your control. There's no better way to learn. Work through the food groups which suit your eating habits - and do so at your own pace.

After comprehensive coverage of food and recipes comes the art of coping with a complete meal. That means preparing a lot of food in a short time without working hurriedly.

You'll find techniques which allow you to go right ahead with almost any basic food, even if it is completely new to you. The last thing you'll bother about will be timings.

Then comes the chapter on how to look after your oven. That doesn't just mean cleaning it. It tells you when to call the engineer, and equally important, it explains circumstances which may cause you to think your oven is faulty when it isn't. That will save you the cost of unnecessary call-outs.

Finally, there is the "Small Print". That's where you can read about certain things in greater detail - should you wish to do so. Technically minded people will love it. Make sure you bring it to the attention of anyone who is that way inclined. It will pay dividends sooner or later.

The Uncertainties

Here are most of the things which can affect foodstuffs and microwave ovens, and alter the way they work together. This affects speed, and makes timings difficult to predict.

THE ACTUAL OVEN POWER
Not all ovens of the same wattage have the same performance. Even if they are the same model, a timing for one may not be quite right for another. Performance can also be affected by soiling of the interior, how hot the oven becomes while it is in use, its age and its condition.

THE ELECTRICITY SUPPLY
The U.K. power supply is nominally 240 volts, with a maximum permitted variation of six per cent. Small variations are not uncommon particularly at times of peak demand, or as a consequence of inadequate or faulty house wiring. Unlike most appliances, microwave ovens can be affected by small changes in supply voltage, and this shows up in the timing.

FOOD TEMPERATURE
This can vary according to freezer, refrigerator and other storage temperatures. The colder the food, the longer it takes.

FOOD MOISTURE CONTENT
Moisture and other constituents can vary, particularly with non-processed foods. This affects timing.

COOKWARE
The mass of a container or cover can extract heat from the food, and cause it to take longer to reach temperature.

In the test kitchens where recommended timings are determined, mains voltage, temperatures and other factors are kept at a normal level. It is impossible to ensure that conditions are the same as that in every home.

Microwave Foods and Browning

As is well known, food can be browned quickly at high temperatures or more slowly at lower temperatures.

Microwave cooks fast at a low temperature, so most foods do not have time to brown. This offers more advantages than disadvantages.

MICROWAVE FOODS WHICH BROWN UNAIDED
Joints of meat - if cooked correctly.
Small cakes, of heavy consistency, such as flapjacks.
Home made breakfast foods and similar substances.
Biscuits, nuts and breadcrumbs.

FOODS WHICH BROWN IN A BROWNING DISH
Steaks, chops, sausages, etc., and most foods which could be cooked conventionally in a frying pan.

FOODS WHICH WOULD BE SPOILED BY A BROWNING EFFECT
Almost everything for de-frosting.
Most things for re-heating.
Most vegetables.
Rice and pasta.
Fruit.
Sauces.
Porridge.
Preserves.
Some puddings.
Some fish dishes.

NON BROWNING IS A DISADVANTAGE mainly with cakes, poultry, and certain made up dishes.

For reasons other than browning, microwave is unsuitable for pastry items in general, or for Yorkshire puddings.

Take up your starting position

People have widely varying views about microwave ovens, so here's something which will help to bring all readers on to an equal footing with regard to attitudes and opinions. Read all the questions and award a point every time you answer yes. Then read what we have to say, just to make sure you are not starting off on the wrong foot.

Q1   To kick off, here's a run up question with no points score. Do you have, or are you thinking of buying just a basic oven?

Q2   Have you made up your mind not to use microwave very much?

Q3   Having tried a number of dishes, would you repeat only those which were a success?

Q4   Would you rather have step by step instructions - and not concern yourself with the whys and wherefores?

Q5   Have you always been sceptical about microwave, and do you still think it may not be worth the effort?

Q6   If you have a combination oven, are you inclined to think that there is no need to learn any of this microwave stuff?

Q7   Would you avoid certain microwave foods because they were pretty awful when cooked at a friend's house?

Q8   Do you use microwave mainly for re-heating and de-frosting?

TOTAL POINTS
The lower the score the better you have done.

Your views reviewed

Here's what we have to say in response to your YES answers - but do read everything even if you said NO.

A1   You should do well. A basic model can cope with most things, and it makes learning easier. Analogue controls (knobs) are a help, so long as the minute marks are reasonably spaced. It is not usually the frills which make a good model, so master your oven before you replace it.

A2   Oh dear! What a pity to impose limitations and deprive yourself of so much. If you examine your reasons, you will probably find a flaw. The best advice is to learn it all, do it all - and then draw the boundaries.

A3   We have all made the mistake of avoiding things which previously failed. It doesn't really make sense, does it? If something turns out badly, always have another go after deciding what went wrong.

A4   Step by step instructions are excellent for some things. No good for learning to ride a bicycle, of course, and not so hot when it comes to microwave. The trouble is, timing can so easily get out of step and foul things up. That's why this is an "understand the stages" book.

A5   Welcome! Experience has shown that many sceptical people become highly enthusiastic. You are probably strong willed, so set your mind to it and look forward to enormous benefits.

A6   People with combination ovens certainly do need to learn about microwave. The same rules and principles apply. A combination oven has extended capabilities, but in the average home, it should still do most of its work as pure microwave.

A7   Yes, to this question is perfectly understandable, but are you blaming the oven instead of the cook? Most people do - but only when it's microwave. The cook will usually say "It can't be my fault, I did precisely what the book said". That's why this book doesn't tell you precisely what to do. It shows you how to manipulate the cooking to suit yourself.

A8   You are one of millions. At last you have the opportunity to get full value from your microwave oven.

Gossip column

Some people never get tired of talking nonsense about microwave ovens, and others innocently repeat it. The most common stories involve "cooking from the inside out", meaning the centre cooks first and the outer parts last. That's easily proved wrong. Simply half cook a potato and cut it open.

Certainly, pie fillings usually end up hotter than the pastry, but that's because of what they are - not where they are. They would still get hotter if they changed places with the pastry. Microwaves find fillings much more attractive than pastry, and favour them with an unfair share of heating power. You'll learn about that sort of thing quite soon.

Microwaves are said to have the disadvantage of not browning food. Most foods don't brown, but it's rarely a disadvantage. On the contrary, microwave owes its great versatility to this non-browning effect. The Foods and Browning chart shows that. We won't dwell on the subject here, it is covered adequately later in the book. For one thing, you'll learn how to ensure that meat browns as it cooks - without colourings or gadgetry.

There are many more stories floating around, but when you've read the book, you'll see right through them.

WHEN IS AN OVEN NOT AN OVEN

When it is microwave, of course. Only a small proportion of its work is "oven" work. Microwave is usually an alternative to the hob, and a very good one too. It will also do things which no ordinary cooker could look at. De-frosting is the obvious example. Never think of your "microwave" as an oven. What a pity it wasn't given a better name at the outset. Some people are still amused when their friends put a cup of coffee into their microwave oven. It is the old image of hot pans, and baking and roasting which does it.

ADVICE TO IGNORE
It has been said many times: don't take microwave advice from friends. Pick up the positive points from their successes, but ignore the warnings following their failures. Your greatest success could be something which failed with them.

SITE IT RIGHT
There are people who almost put their microwave ovens in outhouses, and others who have them down near the floor or at tiptoe height. Needless to say, those ovens are not used much. Have yours at a normal level, where you are in the habit of working, and with plenty of adjacent worktop - so you will have somewhere to put the dishes on their way in and out. Make sure its plug is fitted properly, with its own socket. Do not use an adapter, it may lead to an electrical hazard.

WHAT'S WHAT INSIDE THE OVEN
A microwave oven is a metal box. That's about the only thing which can contain microwaves. You may think yours has a plastic interior, but that's only skin deep on top of the metal. Even the door is a metal wall to microwaves. The metal can have holes in it, as long as they are not too big. The holes can have air blowing through them, and still hold back the microwaves. It's down to the size of the holes, or the see-through wire mesh, so rest assured the designers knew what they were doing.

As long as the door is shut, the box can fill with microwave "radio" energy when you press "start". These cool waves are attracted to any food or liquid in the oven, and having found it, they abandon the microwave life and become heat. There's not a waster among them. Every trace of microwave energy becomes heat somewhere in the "cavity" - the interior.

SCATTERBOX
A very simple metal box oven would work rather badly. Microwaves would tend to congregate in groups and produce uneven heating. It would depend on the shape of the box, the shape of the food, and where it was positioned, etc.. What's needed is something to move the energy around. That's why ovens have a stirrer fan or turntable or rotating antenna. Some models have more than one of these devices. So movement of the energy, or the food, makes for evenness in heating and cooking.

FOOD LEVEL
It is no good just throwing the food into the oven. It must be clear of the metal bottom - or metal tray. Then the energy can spread after it bounces off the metal. That too helps to even out the heating. Some ovens have non-metallic floors with a hidden space beneath. It's the same idea again.

TRAYS
Glass or ceramic trays support the food at a suitable height. Some ovens, particularly combination models (those with added heating elements), have metal trays. They usually have a rack as an extra food support. Always use it with microwave work.

Sometimes food needs to be raised off a glass tray, but that's for a different reason. A container bedded down on the glass surface can cause heat to be leeched from its contents. That can leave food unevenly cooked or heated. The answer is to raise the container off the tray. You can easily demonstrate the effect. Fill a suitable plastic container with water, put it on the tray, and bring the water to the boil. Then see how hot the tray is. The heat in the tray has come from the water - delaying its boiling time.

WATTAGES OLD AND NEW
You may know that your microwave oven has a wattage, and that the higher the wattage, the faster the oven can heat and cook. At this moment, U.K. wattage ratings are changing from the Japanese standard to the European (IEC 705). Until now, home models ranged from below 500 watts, to around 700 watts. In future, ovens will have ratings about 15% higher. It will not mean that they're faster. If you are buying an oven, particularly secondhand, make sure you understand which rating you are being offered - so you know what you are getting for your money.

The good news is that wattages do not affect the procedures described in this book. To a large degree, wattages have to be taken into account only by people who use published timings. It will all make perfect sense as you progress.

CONSUMPTION
Your oven wattage is not the amount of electricity it consumes. Consumption is about twice the "old" wattage, or a bit less than twice the "new' European wattage. For example, an old 600 watt oven (which roughly equals a new 700 watt oven) will consume about twelve hundred watts - when in use on full power.

VARIABLE POWER
This is fully explained later. For now, you need to know only that the oven brings about the variation simply by taking full power, and switching it on and off every few seconds. It then does things more slowly, because it isn't working all the time. On a very low setting it hardly works at all. You can usually hear the effect as a humming sound which comes and goes. It would be a similar situation if you were mowing a lawn and kept stopping for a rest. The job would take longer.

His Master's Dinner

TRADITIONAL
The flame heats the pot
which heats the water
which heats the food

MICROWAVES HEAT FOOD

What the oven does

HOW THE HEATING COMES ABOUT

- The oven fills with microwaves.
- The microwaves find the food and liquid, by seeking out moisture, fat and sugar.
- They change to heat inside it - usually near the surface.
- They ALL become heat, and little is wasted.

Basically, that's it, but you do have to think round it a bit to appreciate what is going to happen to the food. It's to do with energy share. As ALL the microwaves change to heat, the less food there is, the faster it will heat. In other words, SMALLER MEANS FASTER - that sums it up beautifully.

Overlook that, and you may one day look down upon a smouldering mess which you expected to be a tasty snack. It's a common occurrence. Ovens are damaged that way. A small amount goes in, it attracts all the energy, and heats vigorously. The timer hasn't kept up with it, and there's another disaster. SMALLER MEANS FASTER - remember it always.

Energy is shared between the pieces - or numbers of grams or ounces if it's all one piece - it usually amounts to the same thing. That decides how fast the food will heat.

We rarely need to mention wattages, but put two portions in a six hundred watt oven, and they'll have to make do with three hundred watts each - or thereabouts. They get only their share. Heat a bowl containing six hundred peas - and their share will be only about one watt each.

You must admit, that's simple enough, but its altogether different to the way "ordinary" heat behaves. Its so orderly! It makes it perfectly clear that it is no good expecting to use a microwave oven as you would use an ordinary one.

You can now see why smaller amounts cook faster, and larger amounts cook more slowly. So if you wanted to cook food more slowly in a high power oven, you could simply cook more of it - give the oven a bigger "load" - give it more work to do.

On the other hand, if you have to cook a smaller amount and don't want to cook it faster (because that would spoil it), you're going to have to do something to slow down the oven.

It's hardly possible to explain microwave in simpler terms, so do please have it clear in your mind before continuing.

What the oven does

HOT - HOT - HOT
There's an extremely important and quite remarkeable thing about food which has been heated by microwaves. IT STAYS HOT FOR A VERY LONG TIME It's certainly not because it has reached an exceptionally high temperature. In fact, compared with ordinary ovens or fryers, microwave is a low temperature cooker.

It happens because the food has been given a "temperature momentum", a sort of flywheel effect, just like a toy spinning top or gyroscope. Microwaves whip up the heat, and it carries on for ages, just as a top does when the whip is taken away.

This is one of the most useful effects imaginable. Instead of the oven having to work for the whole of the cooking time, it can knock off early, and leave the food to carry on cooking all by itself - somewhere else if necessary.

JUST LOOK AT THE ADVANTAGES

- Two or more things can cook at the same time with only one of them in the oven.

- Food doesn't have to be kept hot - because it doesn't cool for a long time. Even then, it can quickly be heated again.

- The bulkier the piece, the longer it stays hot. So small items have plenty of time to cook in the oven while the bigger things carry on cooking somewhere else.

STANDING TIME
This means the out-of-the-oven cooking time described above.

HOW LONG DOES FOOD REALLY STAY HOT ENOUGH TO SERVE?
It depends on what it is, but a pudding with a four minute cooking time has been known to stay hot for forty minutes. A one minute scrambled egg has stayed hot for eighteen.

The diagram on page 44 shows the overall microwave effect.

That just about covers the main points about microwaves and the way they go to work. We hope you understand them. If you do, you will steer clear of many of the common blunders which regularly cause failure and disappointment.

How you should help it

If you have not, so far, taken in all that has been explained, do please go over it again. It is much more important than you may appreciate at this stage.

PLAY YOUR PART
The microwave oven is amazing, but it doesn't have a brain or a pair of hands. So you must help it by doing the thinking and handling. Given the chance, microwave energy will heat food unevenly, and it's not usually the fault of the oven. No model will evenly heat just anything which is thrown into it, and there may never be one which does.

SHAPES
First, think about the shape of the food or its container.
Round shapes heat most evenly. Where possible, avoid flat or shallow food shapes. They heat more around the edges than in the centre. You might even remove the centre - no centre at all is better than one which is underdone. Remember the effect when heating thick liquids. Use a container small enough to be two thirds full. Stir out from the centre. Whether you are dealing with food or liquid, try to make it as tall as it is wide - within reasonable proportions.

ARRANGING
The "edge effect", described above, applies to arrangements of food as well as to single pieces. Sometimes you can please yourself whether you pile food up or arrange it in a circle. Either will avoid the cool centre of a flat mass.

RE-POSITIONING
Rarely should you leave food standing on the same spot until it is done. Unless you have a turntable, move food around from time to time. Where possible, turn it upside down half way through - even if you do have a turntable.

COVERING
A cover prevents spattering, but it also prevents moisture loss, and holds the heated air so it can be used to advantage. Clingfilm is fine, but it must be the non-toxic microwave type. Lift-off covers make it more convenient to find out what is going on. Throw-away plastic containers or lids will do. They need to be of the thicker more pliable type of material. Not the thin crinkly stuff.

That about takes care of your responsibilities at this stage, and it's not much to ask, is it? As you can see, it's as easy to do things the right way as it is to do them the wrong way.

Getting the food right

SMOOTH THE WAY
If you're using your oven for the first time, or learning new techniques, make sure you have time to think. Give yourself the best possible chance of success.

One thing you need to do instinctively is open the oven door. The door is always the off switch. To stop the energy INSTANTLY, don't panic around the controls - OPEN THE DOOR.

LEARN FROM SUCCESS
When you are enjoying success, note what happened to achieve it, so that you will know that things are going well next time. In particular, remember what the food was like when it began its standing time. We call that the "correctly undercooked" condition, because that's how it should be when it starts its "out of the oven cooking". That's what matters most. You rarely have to consider it in conventional cookery. So it's not surprising that most people are fooled by it when they take up microwave.

Always watch, and check, and remember what you've seen.

SUCCESS FROM FAILURE
If you have just spoiled some food, and we all do that at times, make use of the experience. It may have taught you what not to do, but now decide what must be done for success next time. Don't just throw it into the bin, never to try again. You can hardly be more negative than that, and success comes with being positive.

WHAT WAS THE PROBLEM?
Most likely the food was overcooked, and that's easily recognised. Ask anyone who has eaten bad microwave food. They'll describe it as tough, chewy, stringy, leathery, rubbery or hard as a rock. There are several other possible reasons for poor results, and we have set them out in WHAT WENT WRONG? on page 87. When food is a disappointment, that's where you are likely to find the reason.

TO EVERYONE'S TASTE
By the old methods, microwave food is likely to be right for some people and wrong for others. That's to be expected with predetermined timings. They depend on so many averages. Most food can be cooked to individual taste by microwave, just as it can by other means. It is usually assumed that it can not. What nonsense. Vegetables best illustrate the point, and you will soon be shown how to cook them for results ranging from crunchy to soft.

If hobs had timers, they would also need the timing charts and guides which are normally associated with microwave ovens. People would then bother more about getting timing right than getting the cooking right.

TIMER - FRIEND OR FOE
As the main control on a microwave oven is the timer, it is easy to suppose that timings are a must. In fact, they cause endless problems, so would we be better off without the timer?

If microwave ovens had never had timers, we wouldn't be bothering about what happens in a given number of minutes. Keeping an eye on the oven would be our normal routine, and that would long since have made us experts on what goes on inside it. Knowledge would have been our key to success.

In some circumstances, a timed system is great. Where the work is consistent and repetitive, it is easy to check and adjust timing and there may be no advantage in watching the oven.

Timers often help people do something outside their experience by copying some-one else. An expert does all the donkey work, times every stage, and publishes the timings as part of the instructions. It is later that the uncertainties are encountered, and that's when the system can fall down.

This has been explained to help you to use the timer with discretion, so that it doesn't rule your microwave work, or spoil it. After all, a timer is no more than an on/off switch with a delayed action.

TO TIME OR NOT TO TIME, WHAT IS THE ANSWER?
It is pointless trying to time some things. Milk for example. It is impossible to predict just how long it will take to boil. If the time is always to be the same; quantity, temperature, and several other things will have to be controlled with precision. It can't happen that way. There may be only a couple of seconds between boiling and boiling over, so to catch boiling point you'll just have to watch as it approaches. It's the same with small amounts of scrambled egg, and cup cakes. The only way to get consistent results with things like that is to watch, and whip the door open just at the right moment. Never mind the minutes or the seconds.

This all goes to show that timings are predictions, or if you like, estimates, and inherently chancy. A timing can be dependable when it has been tried, adjusted, tested, and proved on your oven. Not simply on another oven in another location by somebody else, as it is when taken from a book or a package. Find your own timings, and you will take care of many of the uncertainties in the process. Fewer things will be left to chance.

Dispensing with timings

TECHNICAL NECESSITY?
If a microwave oven is started and left to run indefinitely, it will destroy any food which is inside it, and then go on to do itself a mischief. So it is desirable that the oven shall switch off before that can happen, That is the only technical reason for the timer. It is difficult to generalize, but even a mediocre oven should tolerate correct times multiplied by three or four without consequence - if it is clean inside. The complete answer is to keep an eye on your oven.

THE GIFTED FEW
There's nothing new about using microwave without timings. Many caterers keep their timers "wound up" so that they never switch off. They develop an uncanny instinct for opening the door at the right moment. Then there are people who can sense a change in the sound of the oven when the food reaches a certain temperature. If only we could all hear such subtle differences!

GET THE MEASURE OF YOUR OVEN
Put an oven of unknown performance in the hands of a cookery expert, and he or she will probably first heat a cup of water. It's the simplest test of oven performance, and the rule of thumb. It's the first thing you should do when you acquire an oven, and this is how. Take an average size cup and fill it from the cold tap. Test the water with your finger, to see just how cold it is. Heat it on full power for one minute, then test it again. Feel the water, not the cup. Now give it another minute, and test once more. This time it will probably be very hot, but not boiling. Now carry on to see how long it actually takes to boil.

You will easily remember that first experience, and it will enable you to gauge many other things. Half as much water would have heated in about half the time, and twice as much would have taken twice as long. Its a sort of yardstick.

WORKING FREE STYLE
Here's how you can work without timings, or arrive at your own. In previous chapters, you saw that there is no real reason for knowing precisely how long food will take to cook. It will be the same whether you know it in advance or not. You can plan a meal perfectly well with just a rough idea. There's plenty of flexibility, and it doesn't matter if it's ready too soon.

This may sound too free and easy, but it's a highly practical system after a few sessions. You may not yet be ready for elaborate dishes or meals, but you can have a trial run with something basic such as a vegetable.

[CU] the key to successful microwave cookery.

Most cookers have to carry on working until the food is "done to a turn". A microwave oven does not.

Microwaves build up a "temperature momentum" in the food. It then cooks itself to the point of perfection.

So the microwaves must stop while the food is underdone.

The secret of success with microwave cookery is to recognise the correct degree of undercooking, and to stop the microwave energy at that point.

[CU] means CORRECTLY UNDERCOOKED, and it is the symbol which is used throughout this book to denote that key condition.

The new procedures introduced

Basic procedure

KNOW YOUR TARGET
First, look up your chosen food in the Food Section. Check on the **[CU]**

TIE UP THE TIMER
Then ensure that the timer is not going to interrupt. It's no good leaving it at zero, that's obvious, so set it well in excess of the time you expect the job to take. If you think you will need ten minutes, set the timer to twenty. If you're likely to take only two or three minutes, set ten. It really doesn't matter where you start the timer, as long as you choose a convenient round figure, and give yourself plenty of time to get the work done. Note the setting you have chosen.

STAY WITH IT
What you mustn't do, is go away and leave the oven running. This exercise is fun, but you must take it seriously enough to stay with the cooker and keep your mind on what you're doing. If you are urgently called away, just open the oven door before you go. Most foods will be acceptable if you later carry on where you left off, but you will not then have a reliable timing. Shut the oven door, glance to make sure the food is inside, and press START.

CHECK IT
Based on your crude estimate of the cooking time, open the door a quarter of the way through. See what the food is like. It shouldn't yet be the way you want it, so carry on.

SATISFY YOURSELF
Make further checks at reasonable intervals until the food is correctly undercooked - **[CU]**

The new procedures introduced

STAND IT
The food should stand for at least as long as it has already taken. Then check that it is cooked to your satisfaction.

THE PROVED TIMING
See how far the timer has run down from the original setting, and there is your tested and proved timing.

If the result is not to your liking, here's what you do. Decide whether it is undercooked, overcooked, or wrong in some other way. Find the answer in What Went Wrong on page 87 and perhaps revise your idea of [CU].

Here's an example of the procedure.

- Jacket potato in oven.   Timer setting   10 min.
- [CU] is slightly firm in centre, crinkly skin.
- First check   hot, steaming and hard.
- Second check   still too hard
- Third check   as [CU]
- Potato to stand   Timer now at   4 min.
-                                       Cooking time   6 min.

WHAT YOU HAVE ACHIEVED

1 The result, with a good chance of perfection.

2 A tested and proved timing.

3 Experience. You're getting the idea of using the procedure which, with practice, becomes effortless

Next, you will do well to master srambled egg, so look that up in the food section and have a go. Use the jug recommended, not a larger one, that would make the egg too shallow. It will cook more evenly with a better depth. Use a fork.

What variable power is

YOUR PROSPECTS
You'll be able to cook almost anything using this alternative procedure. It's for re-heating and de-frosting too. If you normally work alongside your cooker, it can be your regular system. Thousands of people already work that way.

If your work is repetitive, you will be able to use your timer to best advantage with your own list of individual timings. They will be more dependable than others.

When you are faced with something you've never cooked before, you'll be able to go right ahead with it. Please read on, you're not yet ready for any more cooking.

VARIABLE POWER - WITHOUT THE CONTROL
Before we come to the power control, consider how the power always adjusts itself automatically. It brings us back to SMALLER MEANS FASTER.

Let's say you want to reduce power for a jacket potato, because you prefer the slow cooked result. You could simply cook two instead of one. You know they'll take longer, but had you seen that as slower cooking? Not everone does. Yet it's just the same as reducing the power level. With a casserole, you could double up on the quantity and maybe improve that with slower cooking. It's a useful technique if you don't have variable power. Not often practical perhaps, but it illustrates an important principle.

THE VARIABLE POWER CONTROL
You saw what the control did, when we went over the oven bits. Now you can see what's wrong with the way it's so often used. A fixed setting is expected always to have a certain effect, ignoring the fact that it will vary with the amount of food.

If the oven had a mind, it would be thoroughly confused by all this. One week the control gives it medium/high power to use on a four pound joint. The next week it gives it the same for a two pound joint. No wonder the oven gets into trouble, it has to use all that energy on half as much meat, and that means working twice as fast. That quickly gets the joint into a boiling rage, with no chance of becoming browned off.

What variable power does

> ### SHORT TIME TIP
> Do not use variable power if the oven is to run for less than one minute. That's how long it takes most controls to "shape" the energy to the level selected. If, for example, you were to run the oven for only ten or fifteen seconds at medium power, you might get full power, or you might get nothing at all. It's the way with nearly all variable power controls, but it need not bother you.
>
> The answer is to apply full power in short bursts. Just open the door every six to eight seconds as necessary. It is easy to do and it suits our way of working. Try it on some stale bread, you'll soon get the hang of it.

THINK OF A GAS FLAME

This is an easy way to understand variable power, and it makes it crystal clear that power levels are not temperatures. Everybody knows that a large flame will boil water faster than a small one. That's familiar everyday stuff, so just think of your variable power as a flame turning up and down, and you'll have a pretty good idea of the effect it is having.

We all know that water boils fast if there's not much of it. In the microwave oven, it's the same with food and cooking.

Compare the two ideas, altering the flame, and altering the amount. Either will affect the time needed to do the heating. With microwave, it can be the time needed to do the cooking.

So power levels cannot be temperatures. Boiling is a temperature, the smallest flame will boil water, and so will the lowest power level in a microwave oven.

What variable power does

POWER LEVELS WITH NAMES
Lots of microwave ovens have power levels with names such as Simmer, Roast, etc.. Lets take Simmer. Clearly, the quantity of liquid will have to be right if that setting is just going to simmer it. Have too much and it won't, and the power will have to be shifted up to another level, perhaps "Roast"!

The explanation is that these "Guide Levels" were introduced a long time ago, to help a public who new nothing about microwave ovens . The levels did make sense. They were about right for average amounts, as cooked by average people. Having fulfilled their original purpose, these guides have unfortunately been taken too literally, and have given rise to misconceptions.

The one setting which can suit varying amounts is "De-frost". You will see why that is different when you come to the chapter on de-frosting.

ROAST BEEF OF THE SEVENTIES
Before we leave Guide Levels, lets look at the "Roast" setting, and its history. Variable power first appeared in the mid seventies, and Roast was fixed at a level to suit the average British joint. In those days its weight was about four pounds, and the guide setting was chosen to ensure a cooking time in excess of twenty minutes. A joint needs that sort of time if it is to be tender and brown. Had the average joint have been smaller, a lower setting would have been chosen.

...AND THE NINETIES?
Now, of course, the average joint is very much smaller, but the roast setting is still used, together with the old faithful minutes per pound chart. In no time at all, the tiny joint comes out looking boiled, and sometimes as tough as old boots - brown boots if colourings are used. It will not always be that bad, of course. It depends on the quality of the meat.

What variable power does

So what's wrong with the minutes per pound chart so familiar to traditional cooks? Nothing, where traditional cooking is concerned, but this is microwave. It's so fast with small amounts that cooking times are hopelessly inadequate for a roasting joint. Prescribed power levels and minutes per pound obscure the fact that cooking varies with weight.

Our food chapters show how to cook all types of meat without running into any of the problems just described.

IT'S THE WRONG LINK
In this book, we say (frequently) that SMALLER MEANS FASTER. Usually though, smaller simply means a shorter time, and the increased cooking speed is not considered. So the powerful link between amount and time is the cause of endless problems.

When dealing with sizeable quantities of food, you will need full power, except for de-frosting. Your oven will not have enough power to cook too quickly, so it is right to match the time to the amount. When you do have to reduce power (except for de-frosting), consider matching that to the food quantity. Alter the amount - alter the power. More for more, less for less. This is a logical way of using microwave energy for cooking, making power levels less like temperatures

HALF-RECIPES
If a recipe calls for reduced power, it means full power would be too FAST for a good result. It is not a question of temperature. If you cook only half the quantity without further reducing the power, you'll lose the benefit of the original power reduction.

It has become standard practice to reduce cooking time for half-recipes, it's that mental link again. With vegetable dishes, that may be for the best. Faster cooking may enhance the result. Meat is a different matter, so do what you would do with a smaller joint, and reduce the power. Aim to maintain the original recipe time. That's what matters.

De-frosting

OVEN DE-FROST POWER

This does not mean Auto de-frost. That is explained on page 36.

"De-frost" is a general purpose level which is about right for one average piece of food. It is not ideal for everything, nor is it a magic level which can de-frost without being able to heat or cook.

The word "De-frost" against a switch or a variable control may lead you to think otherwise. It is not possible to say which level is best, without knowing what food is to be de-frosted. Even then the only way to be certain is to observe the de-frosting process, and make "fine tuning" adjustments for best results.

Microwaves cannot instantly enter frozen food, so at first, they work like crazy on its surface. High power can spoil the outer parts before reaching the inner parts. Low power will not, and two hundred watts suits the average piece of food. That's around medium/low on variable power. At lower levels, de-frosting simply takes longer, and time is wasted. If that doesn't matter, then there is no disadvantage.

Beginners should use de-frost level or lower, depending on how de-frosting progresses, even for a large piece of food. **Never be tempted to use high power just because you are in a hurry.** You can hardly expect the oven or the food to behave differently because you are short of time. The de-frosting process must take as long as is necessary for safe results.

De-frosting

WHEN TO DROP BELOW DE-FROST POWER

If a certain food gets more than a little warm before it has de-frosted through, your de-frost level is too high for it. If the oven has no lower level, keep interrupting it. That will reduce the power for sure. Alternatively, de-frost two pieces of food together (not one piece twice the size). That is the same as reducing the power level.

This advice applies particularly to delicate foods such as cream cakes. With those it may be necessary to do three or four at a time to thin out the energy. Prawns to be eaten cold are another example of a food requiring slower de-frosting. Remember to shake things like that around once or twice to prevent hot spots on the parts which protrude.

Those are the basic guidelines which concern the oven and the levels. You also need to know something about food peculiarities. That information is in the food chapters. See page 48.

More efficient de-frosting

A DE-FROST TECHNIQUE FOR THE EXPERIENCED WORKER

Important. This is not suitable for beginners.

This is basically the idea which was used with the cream cakes, when two or more of them shared de-frost power to weaken its effect. Here, two or more portions share a higher level. That's better than de-frost power between them. This is a very efficient method. Three or four portions can de-frost as quickly as one, with each receiving no more than ordinary de-frost power.

That's how it works, and this is how you do it:

Before you can use this technique, you must be familiar with the way one portion of food normally reacts to de-frost power.

- Make sure the portions are roughly equal, and that there is more than one in the oven.

- Select a power level which will allow each portion up to a quarter of full power, e.g. half power for two portions.

- Proceed with the de-frosting, checking from time to time to see that progress is normal. If it is not, adjust the power up or down as necessary.

- Stop when the food is sufficiently de-frosted, and rest it in the usual way.

Thorough checking is the key to all successful de-frosting. Remember that at every stage of the process and you can hardly go wrong.

This method cannot be applied to a single mass, however large. It relies on division of energy between a number of similar pieces. The only way to shorten the de-frost time for a large piece of food, is to break it into smaller pieces, preferably all the same size. Then you can increase the power.

ALL DE-FROSTING TECHNIQUES NEED CARE AND ATTENTION

Perfect de-frosting

HOW TO TELL WHEN FOOD IS DE-FROSTED
It is easy enough to distinguish between a piece of food which is frozen, and another piece which is not. It is different when you have food which was still frozen a short time earlier, and you have to decide whether it has thawed completely. Ideally, you check its temperature at several points, but few people are equipped to do that.

The usual way is to feel it, prod it, spear it, pull it apart or take some other action which will show beyond doubt that it is well above freezing point throughout.

Don't keep the microwave energy going until that standard is reached. Depending on the type of food, it is sometimes desirable, even essential, to have ice crystals left in the food as it begins its de-frost standing time. It may also be warm in places, perhaps with small hot spots. The purpose of de-frost standing time is to allow these extremes of temperature to even out, so that the whole mass is then as it would be if it had come from a refrigerator.

Only experience will show you what is normal during the de-frost process, which includes standing time. Common sense will tell you what the food should be like at the end of it. Remember that it can be risky, with regard to bacteria, to begin cooking or re-heating food which is not fully de-frosted.

SPECIAL DE-FROST FEATURES
"Auto de-frost" provides power which is automatically reduced in steps, and extends into what would normally be the standing time. It is a feature of ovens which can be set so that de-frost is followed immediately by heating or cooking. Use it only in accordance with manufacturer's instructions and be very careful if you decide to experiment with it. Ovens with this feature can still de-frost the ordinary way.

"Computer de-frost" uses electronics to make calculations and set its own time. It may base that time on only two things; the type of food and its weight. Knowing no more than that, it cannot take other variable factors into account: food temperature, for example. So it cannot be expected always to arrive at the ideal de-frosting time. After all, it is only using a list of suggested times in its memory, to save you the trouble of reading them off paper. If it frequently gives poor results, do the de-frosting in the normal way. A possible reason for lack of success is an abnormal freezer temperature. All freezers and refrigerators should be checked from time to time using a suitable thermometer.

Perfect re-heating

RE-HEATING
Never risk causing confusion by calling this cooking. Food for re-heating is already cooked. A good general rule is that food should be either cold, as from the refrigerator, or piping hot. Some foods must never be kept warm, or served warm, meat dishes in particular.

With re-heating, you must pay attention to most of the things which apply to cooking. Shape, arrangement, re-positioning, stirring, covering, and so on. Then avoid overheating and allow standing time.
Most important, check temperature.

WHAT IS RIGHT?
To be absolutely certain about serving temperature, you must use a thermometer, and ensure that all parts of the food rise above 70°C for at least two minutes. So don't just stick the thermometer in one place, and take that to be the temperature throughout. With slapdash use of microwave, food can be both boiling and cold - in the same small dish.

Without a thermometer, you'll have to learn to use judgement, and your fingers. The back of a finger is probably the most suitable and convenient heat sensor we carry around with us. To give you something to go on, most people like their hot drinks at around 60°C, and that's a lot cooler than 70°C. Remember the "edge effect" with food which is lying flat. Be sure to check the temperature at its centre.

OVERHEATING
Microwave can re-heat food superbly, retaining all the colour and flavour, but it slightly alters the texture of some things. For example, flaky pastry will become softer. You have already learned what overcooking does: overheating spoils food in the same way. Sugary things will first caramelize, then smoke, burn, and perhaps flame. It is essential that you practice re-heating food in order to be able to do it perfectly.

GUIDELINES FOR PERFECT RE-HEATING
It is not possible to give specific advice about re-heating every conceivable item of food. Here are the main points, and the rest is a matter of paying attention to what you are doing. USE FULL POWER, except with very small or delicate items of food, or anything else which may benefit from slower re-heating. Food must already be fully cooked. Half cooked food, particularly meat and poultry, can contain dangerous bacteria.
The exception would be a blanched vegetable system, where cooking is completed on re-heating.

Perfect re-heating

Light textured foods, such as sponge puddings, heat very quickly indeed. You may need to check after thirty seconds.
Use a cover to retain moisture, except for "dry" foods such as pies, pizzas, danish pastries, etc.. Things like that should stand on a rack or kitchen paper, to prevent sogginess.

Be sure to let the food stand, e.g. a minute or two for a plated meal, and up to FIVE MINUTES for four portions of lasagne. This ensures thorough heating, and improves quality.

Never re-heat food more than once.
It can be dangerous.

Liquids should be stirred when they leave the oven. Be careful if they are nearly boiling, they can gush out on being stirred. Stir sauces and custards every two minutes or so, using a whisk, it prevents lumps. Use a bowl with a rounded base, and for casseroles too. Higher power can be used where stirring is frequent. The interruptions are equal to a power reduction.

Check VEGETABLES frequently. Add a knob of butter for better results. With mashed or pureed vegetables, stir when there is any sign of drying round the edges.

MEAT, FISH and CHICKEN portions should be turned if possible. Reduce power with small amounts of fish. If necessary, make a slit in the centre of a portion for a final temperature check.

PASTRY need not spoil on re-heating. Flaky pastry pies containing a lot of gravy or fruit, are tricky. Avoid them. The shorter the pastry the better it re-heats. Remove foil containers. Do not place the food on a cold solid surface, use a rack of some kind. Make a hole in pastry tops. A cloud of steam is often a sign of overheating. Never use a cover, make the usual temperature checks, and REST to restore texture.

In general then, stir everything which can be stirred, turn things over where possible. MAKE ABSOLUTELY CERTAIN FOOD IS HOT, by giving it AS LONG AS IT TAKES TO GET IT RIGHT.

Christmas food problems

GOODBYE TO YULE-TIDE BLUNDERS

Christmas pudding and mince pies are ruined every year by overheating. Yet it is so easy to get them right.

CHRISTMAS PUDDING: Cut a whole pudding into portions, and splay them out so that they do not touch each other. Cover with an OVERSIZED bowl. Heat on full power for JUST ONE MINUTE. Remove from the oven and examine. Repeat this until VERY NEARLY HOT ENOUGH.
Then allow to stand for a short while. This procedure cannot fail. The interruptions equal a power reduction - which is ideal. For SINGLE PORTIONS, check after THIRTY SECONDS, or reduce power to extend re-heating time.

MINCE PIES: DO SEVERAL AT A TIME, or reduce power. WATCH THEM. They will be hot enough when the pastry is JUST WARM. On full power, they may need no more than twenty seconds per mince pie.

GET THE WATER RIGHT

In conventional cookery, water sometimes has to carry the heat to the food - as with the vegetables in the pot, at the front of the book. There is no need for that in a microwave oven. The purpose of the water is to ensure that the food is moist when cooked. Some water evaporates, and ideally, you'd finish up with none to spare. It's difficult to estimate the quantity as accurately as that so aim to have a little left over. Beginners can follow a cookbook for quantity. Ensure that the water is dispersed around the food. With cabbage, for example, don't put the water down the bottom and dry leaves on top. They'll probably dehydrate and discolour long before the water vapour can reach them. Shake the water around with the food.

Cookware and browning dish

COOKWARE
Essentially, this should be unaffected by microwave energy or hot food, particularly fats and sugars, and it must be as light as possible. Where the food will take the shape of its container, a round one will be best, and one with a good depth, to minimise the edge effect described earlier. Reserve rectangular dishes for food which keeps its own shape.

HEAVYWEIGHT CONTAINERS
Food in a heavy container takes longer to heat, because it is continuously losing heat to the container. Water can take three times as long to boil in a large stoneware dish, compared with a glass tumbler. That doesn't mean you should avoid such dishes. They can enhance results, and they look good too.

UNNECESSARY FROZEN MASS
A heavy container frozen with the food can be a problem.
De-frosting can be difficult if there is as much dish as there is food. It all has to come up to temperature.

THE BROWNING DISH
This is the microwave frying pan. The dish in the oven is as the pan on the hob - with the addition of microwave cooking. The dish does more than just heat to brown the food. By taking its share of energy, it reduces cooking speed. That's usually ideal for browning dish type food.

A browning dish is the only sort which can be heated alone in a microwave oven. Be familiar with the pre-heating instructions for your dish. Never cook a joint of meat in it. You'll see the reasons when you learn about meat in the food chapters.

TEMPERATURE PROBES AND MICROWAVE THERMOMETERS
These have a number of uses, one of which is to sense the internal temperature of a joint to indicate when it has had enough cooking. That's much better than trying to use your own judgment, or cutting the joint open to find out. There is no effect on the way the meat cooks, so even with an oven probe, you must "stretch" the cooking time for small joints. A probe or thermometer detects when the joint is done enough, but the power level decides when it is to happen. Thermometer instructions may not mention this, so perhaps all joints are big where they originated.

Probes are not used the same way in all makes and models of microwave oven. You need to find out whether variable power still works when your

Probes, thermometers and sensors

probe is in use. If it doesn't, you can not use the probe with our small joint procedure.

A probe can be very useful with hot drinks and casseroles.

"Heat and hold" brings food or liquid up to a selected temperature and maintains it. It is a thermostat. It may work at full power regardless of the setting on the power control. Never use it for cooking meat in the shape of a joint. It is best for moist and bulky made up dishes, and liquids.

OVEN SENSOR COOKING

You could say that you needn't know so much if you use a sensor.
True, but who wants to do everything by sensor? Sensors often succeed as a sales feature and are never used. They do have their uses - so why not take advantage?

The simplest sensor is the temperature probe which has just been described.

Infra-red sensors detect the food surface temperature, and they can control a complete cooking procedure. They determine the amount of food by knowing that smaller means faster, and adjust power levels in line with procedures used in this book.

Most sensors are the humidity type, but one sort sniffs the food. As with infra-red, the sensing is usually done in the first few minutes. The electronics then calculate a cooking and standing time.

All sensors must be used in accordance with instructions. With the humidity or aroma types, the oven door must not be opened during the first stage. That's when the sensor is working.

Combination ovens

These are microwave ovens which are also a conventional oven or grill or all three. They are sometimes looked upon as highly developed microwave ovens, their conventional facilities being regarded as microwave oven features. That is not really so.

It is often said that it would be wonderful to have one cooker to do absolutely everything, but if that included every type of cooking in common use, it would often prove impractical. Most households would need at least two, and that would defeat the object. It is unlikely that any cooker will ever be able to cope with such widely varied work at any one time, or within a reasonable meal preparation period.

Microwave rules are unaltered for cookers which incorporate non-microwave features. The basic principles apply equally to combination ovens, except, of course, when they are being used in a non-microwave mode. "Combination mode" uses a set temperature, plus microwave energy. Temperature holds good for any size load, but as you know, microwave power does not. With widely varying amounts of food, this can mean inconsistent results. If the variable power facility is available in combination mode, adjustments can be made to compensate. If it is not, it is advisable to adhere to the manufacturer's tested food quantities, or their equivalent.

The most popular combination is microwave and convection oven. Here, convection means heat forced around by a blower instead of circulating naturally. This improves efficiency by shifting cool air which would otherwise shroud the food.

If you own a combination oven, you may be neglecting the microwave mode. This could be because you've never been entirely convinced of the

Combination ovens

value of pure microwave.
The advantages of combination ovens are that they save space, can cost less than separate cookers, and can give excellent results with microwave assisted oven cooking.

With some exceptions, very similar results can be achieved by using two separate cookers, microwave followed by convection. That is better for the microwave meal sequence, and it obviates the need for hob back-up. Neither cooker has do the work of the other. Both can be used at one time, and for different purposes. Microwave stays cool running and easy to clean. Hot oven can have a full self-cleaning interior, and greater shelf space. If one goes wrong, the other is there to the rescue .

Combination ovens are an attractive concept. They incorporate what microwave can be thought to lack. The ideal set up might well be pure microwave plus a combination oven. That will truly give the best of both worlds.

THE MICROWAVE COOKING PROCESS

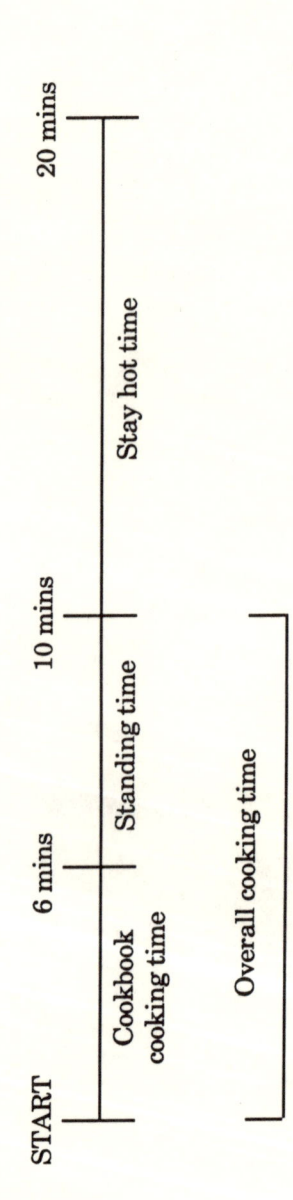

```
START    6 mins        10 mins              20 mins
  |--------|--------------|--------------------|
  Cookbook  Standing time      Stay hot time
  cooking time
  |-----------------------|
      Overall cooking time
```

These proportions are typical, but foods vary considerably. Puddings, for example, may stay hot for ten times as long as their oven cooking time.

Foods and recipes

By the time you have worked around to this point, you should feel happy to tackle any basic food. If this is not so, back-pedal a little, and be patient. Reading alone can never make a cook. There really is no substitute for experience.

Lets consider the complete meal. You may once have wanted to cook several foods together as in conventional cookery. It will now be obvious that there is no point in doing that. How on earth could you get the energy to sort itself out around all the different shapes and sizes and substances. Everything would cook so slowly that results would be inferior with some of the food. You'll be lucky to get good results if you copy the popular microwave demonstration which uses concentric circles of different vegetables. It's a job to balance them so each one cooks to best advantage. Vegetables cook better in small quantities, or simple combinations.

It may not seem so, but the microwave meal plan is little different to that used in conventional cookery. Either way, the foods have to be cooked in the right sequence to arrive at the table as and when required. What may have fooled you is that microwave food cooks without being in the cooker all the time. If something is out of sequence, you can soon catch up; or if it has cooled, you can quickly make it hot again.

FIRST TIME
At your very first attempt at a meal, cook most of it conventionally. Just do a microwave vegetable. Next time do two. Then gradually build up to a complete meal. Expect to spoil something occasionally, that's how you'll learn.

Foods and recipes

THE COMPLETE MEAL
The secret of success is to do things in the right sequence, starting with the largest and most bulky food. When that is out of the oven, cooking and keeping hot, you'll often have more than enough time to do the rest. Look at the accompanying illustration of the meal sequence. Note its four stages. They are all equally important.

PLANNING AND PREPARATION
Decide exactly what you're eating, and when. Rule out new recipes and other things you've never done before. Get any de-frosting underway. Have all dishes and ingredients to hand before you start. If you are going to need something part-cooked at a later stage, this is when you part-cook it. Leave shellfish, cheese or egg dishes until last. They need very little standing time, and do not re-heat well.

MAIN COOKING
Select your bulkiest item, and start cooking it. Potatoes usually come second, as for example when the main dish is chicken; but if it is fish, the potatoes would be cooked first. Thin fish fillets would follow all the vegetables, which too should be in their right sequence according to bulk. Class corn on the cob as bulky, as it is exceptionally good at staying hot. There's no need to do all the preparation before you start the cooking. Do it as you go along, while successive items are cooking in the oven - or cooking out of it - or staying hot.

STANDING COOKING
So each item has reached [CU], and is cooking or staying hot on the worktop along with the rest. Now you can drain the vegetables, and add any seasonings or butter. Stir liquids, sauces, casseroles or stews. Loosely cover foods where appropriate. If you wish to prolong the staying hot; meat, poultry and jacket potatoes can be wrapped in aluminium foil, but this is by no means a necessity. Check the food well before it is due at the table, and if anything is underdone, return it to the oven right away. You'll rarely need to do this if you have worked according to the guidelines.

STAYING HOT UNTIL SERVED
This is where you will appreciate the flexibility of the system. Now perhaps, you can re-heat gravy or sauce - not forgetting to stir. Last of all, carve the meat. What about the pudding? With experience, you could start to cook it at this late stage, or if it is a very fast one, even later. Otherwise, you will have cooked it in sequence earlier, or have one ready for re-heating as you clear the main course. That way it won't matter if no-one wants any. That's the general idea. Now try one of our suggested menus before you go entirely ad lib.

THE MICROWAVE MEAL SEQUENCE

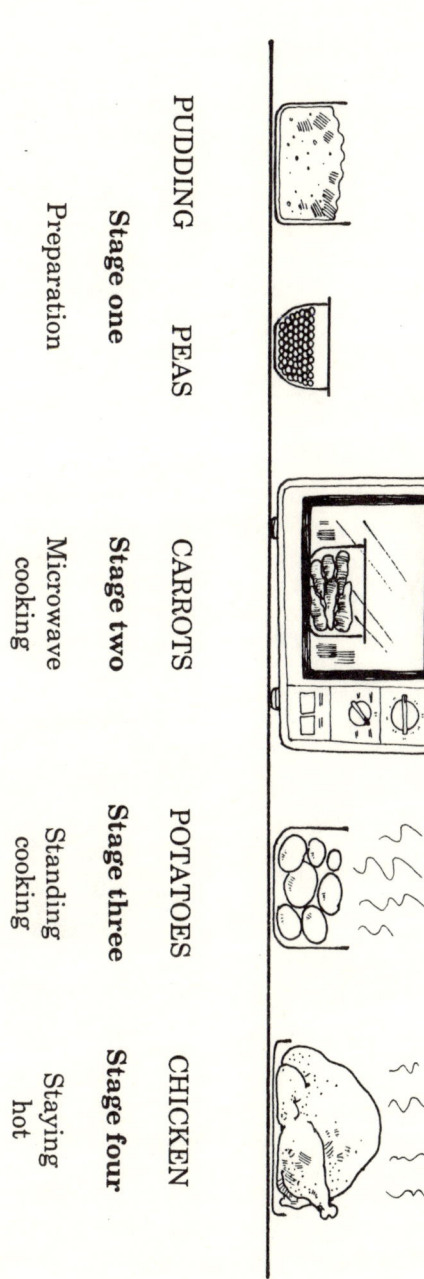

PUDDING	PEAS	CARROTS	POTATOES	CHICKEN
Stage one		**Stage two**	**Stage three**	**Stage four**
Preparation		Microwave cooking	Standing cooking	Staying hot

47

THE DE-FROSTING PROCESS
The procedures have already been explained, so this is all to do with the food itself.
Loosen all wrappings, and remove everything in the way of labels, ties, etc.. Everything. Put the food into a microwave-safe container which fits it, and cover loosely.

If the food is in a mass which can be broken down, or separated, or turned over, attend to it as soon as it becomes a possibility. For example, take a fork to a lump of mince as soon as it can be broken up. It is no good expecting a quick result with a big thick piece of food in one lump. It may take ages by microwave standards, although it is sometimes unavoidable.

Re-arranging food always helps, and the more often, the better.

Be sure to notice any signs of cooking, and take appropriate action as advised earlier. Obviously, overheating and part cooking indicates power too high. The immediate remedy is to rest the food for a while.

If you are a really careful worker, you can use little pieces of aluminium foil to shield small areas of the food which are vulnerable to overheating whilst de-frosting. Fish tails, chicken wings and tops of breastbones are examples.

RULES FOR USING ALUMINIUM FOIL

- Use only small pieces of foil.
- Make sure there is plenty of exposed food to take up the energy.
- Make sure the foil never goes close to the oven walls or door.

Remove the foil at around half time to allow the energy to reach the parts which have been shielded.

PREPARING FOOD FOR THE FREEZER
Careful planning at this stage will make de-frosting much easier. Make sure the food is well cooked, then chill it quickly. Freeze in either the cooking/serving dish or one of similar size, and preferably not a heavy one. Avoid having pieces of food protruding, out of frozen sauce for instance. Food in boiling bags should be frozen lying flat. With plated meals, make sure every piece of food in them is fully cooked, and pay attention to correct layout. Home frozen food takes longer to de-frost than commercially frozen food. That's because it contains larger ice crystals.

POWER LEVEL EQUIVALENTS GUIDE

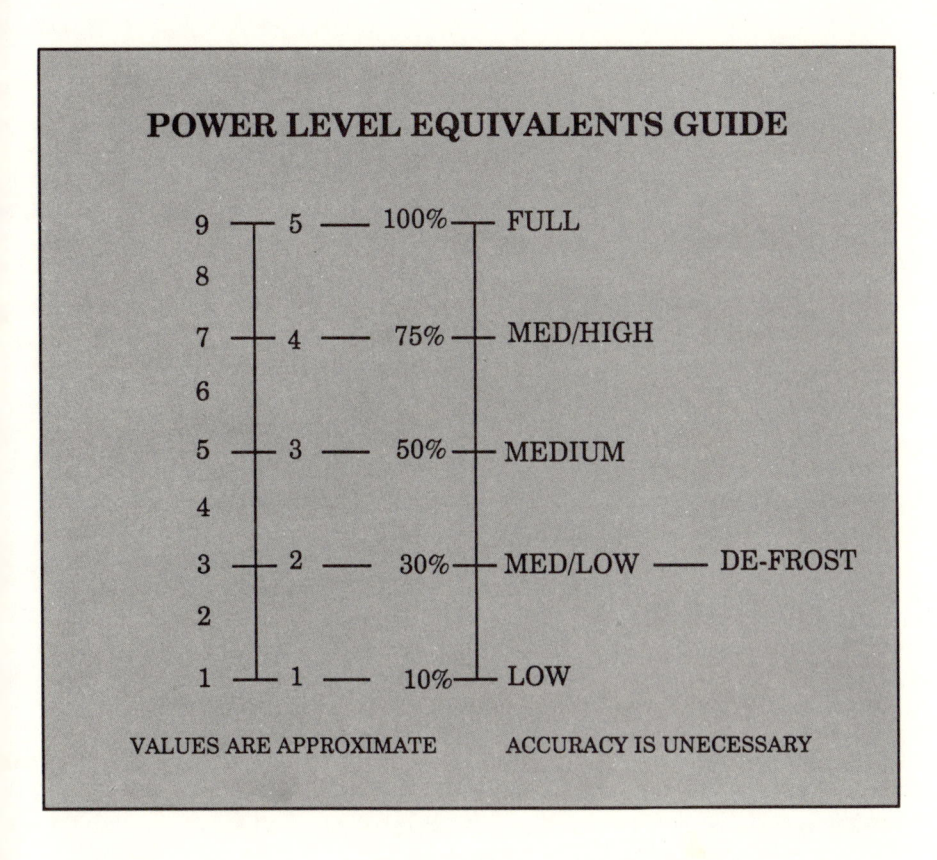

9	5	100%	FULL
8			
7	4	75%	MED/HIGH
6			
5	3	50%	MEDIUM
4			
3	2	30%	MED/LOW — DE-FROST
2			
1	1	10%	LOW

VALUES ARE APPROXIMATE   ACCURACY IS UNECESSARY

POWER FOR POWER

Power levels are regrettably not standarized. In this book, we give them simple descriptive names. Our full power is high, or 100% or whatever the top number may be on your oven. We hope the other levels will be equally obvious from the above diagram; but remember, there is no need for accurate settings - not while you are following our methods.

Cooking in earnest

One of the obvious things about microwave ovens is that they all have see-through doors. Unfortunately, most microwave cooks regard the door as a barrier between themselves and the food until it is (hopefully) done enough.

Having gone along with the book so far, you will know the folly of that sort of relationship with the food. To be consistently successful, you'll have to stay better in touch with it than that. Take the word touch literally. In addition to the stirring, turning, shifting and shielding, you'll often need to lay a clean finger on the food to find out whether all is well. You will then know whether it is hot, cold, hard, soft, wet or dry. They are the things which will tell you that it is right.

Food will retain its natural colour until it is cooked, and some of it can be made to take long enough for a colour change. That's great, but it still leaves a few foods in need of cosmetic aid. With faster cooking meat items such as chops, pre-grilling can add colour. Certain other foods can have their standing time under the grill, and that can give them the traditional finish. Your cook book may offer other ideas for enhancing appearances.

On the next page is one of the foods which does brown and crisp naturally when cooked by microwave. You'll enjoy it for breakfast, or sprinkled on ice cream.

BREAKFAST FOOD

Muffet Crunch

allow 10 minutes, plus cooling time. Use a large shallow dish.

175g (6ozs) rolled oats
75g (3ozs) bran
50g (2ozs) shredded or desiccated coconut
50g (2ozs) sunflower seeds
60g (2½ozs) unsalted butter
30g (1½ozs) oil
150g (5ozs) honey

Optional but preferable: walnuts, hazelnuts, brazil nuts, dried fruit.

Combine all ingredients except nuts and fruit, and spread evenly over the dish. Cook on full power, stirring several times.
[CU] the mixture is brown and has lost its stickiness. Allow to cool, stirring occasionally.
When cold, add the nuts and/or fruit, and transfer to an airtight container.

VEGETABLES
If you like your vegetables just so, be particular about quality and freshness when you buy them. To cook, wash them well, removing woody stems, dehydrated leaves, spots and discolouration. Select or piece into uniform sizes, and arrange in an even pattern; head to tail if necessary. Arrange the larger vegables in a circle. Peas, chopped vegetables and suchlike should go into small bowls, to give depth to the food.

All need added water, except jacket potatoes and corn on the cob in its husk. How much, will depend on how dry they are. Mushrooms spinach, beansprouts and spongy Brussels sprouts, will hold enough water just from the rinsing. A cauliflower will need four to eight tablespoons. The amount of water will affect the final texture, especially with boiled potatoes. So experiment until you are happy. If you are going to mash the potatoes, cook with extra water. Loosely cover vegetables for cooking, except jacket potatoes.

It is easy to dress up vegetables with a sauce, or crunchy browned almonds with butter, or browned breadcrumbs with chopped herbs. You can simply shake them around with a knob of butter when they have reached [CU].

Vegetables

If you are an absolute beginner, make your first check at around half the cooking time given in your cookbook, but remember, that is the only use you will have for the cookbook time. Do the necessary stirring or shaking, and carry on cooking, but this time, not for so long, then check again.

[CU] Be guided by these descriptions:

- just hard in the centre when tested with a knife blade;
- when squeezed, skin almost bursting, flesh coming through;
- not quite done enough when sampled and eaten.

This remember, is when the microwave energy must stop. Put the vegetables back for more and they will spoil. To satisfy personal taste, try cooking less, or cooking faster or slower, or just push standing time to the limit.

Now you can drain them, add butter if you wish, and let them stand, covered, for at least half the time they have cooked, and up to four times as long. Always check the final result.

Use a similar technique to cook vegetables right from frozen.

Vegetables can be cooked in certain combinations. Cut them all to the same smallish size, or add small to large as you go along. You will not succeed if you try to do big quantities.

Next is a delicious recipe which will also serve as a guide to combination vegetable cookery. We are not referring to combination ovens.

Chinese Vegetables

Serves 4-5   Use 2 litre (3 pint) casserole dish.
Allow 15mins. plus 5mins. standing.

green pepper, sliced
red pepper, sliced
1 small onion, finely sliced
175g (6oz) broccoli florets
100g (4oz) button mushrooms, sliced
1 tbsp cornflower
2 tbsp soy sauce
2 tbsp dry sherry
150ml ($1/_4$ pint) chicken stock
100g (4oz) beansprouts

Place peppers, onion, and broccoli in dish and shake around with 4 tbsp water. Cook covered until onion is opaque. Stir in mushrooms and cook until just softening, then add beansprouts. Blend cornflour with soy sauce, sherry and chicken stock, add to other ingredients and stir well. Cook on full power until boiling, stirring several times to prevent sticking. Then stand.

Fruit

Savoury Stuffed Peppers

Serves 4   Use 20cm (8inch) shallow dish and 1.75 litre (3 pint) bowl
Allow 20 mins. plus 5 mins

4 medium green peppers
1 tbsp oil
1 onion, finely chopped
200g (7 oz) cooked weight, brown rice
1 large courgette, grated
2 tomatoes, chopped
100g (4 oz) red Leicester cheese
salt and pepper
150ml (5 fl. oz) vegetable stock or single cream

Cut off the tops of the peppers and keep them to use as caps. Remove centres and seeds. Moisten the peppers with water. Using full power all along, first heat the peppers in the dish, covered, until they are very hot. Then allow to stand, with cover removed. Cook the onion in the bowl with the oil until it is slightly softened, then stir in the rest of the ingredients and check the seasoning. Fill the peppers with this mixture and put on their caps.
[CU] Fillings well heated through, and peppers slightly soft. Allow to stand, covered, for five minutes.

FRUIT

Choose ripe fruit of good quality. Wash it, and where appropriate, remove skins, stalk, etc.. If poaching or "baking" whole fruit, match sizes for even results.

If slicing, slice evenly. Speed of cooking varies with different fruits, so it is better not to cook mixtures.

Cook whole fruit in a dish filled but not crowded. Fruit with skins can have a sugar or honey topping, or it can be cooked in a syrup, wine or fruit juice mixture. Use full power. Fillings sometimes foam out of apples. Never mind that, they can always be spooned back later.

For sliced fruit, use enough water just to moisten. Cook covered, on full power, until boiling. Stir, and cook until softened. Add any sugar after cooking. Alternatively, cook the fuit in a sugar syrup. Use a large dish for rhubarb, as it tends to foam.

Fruit

Cook dried fruit in $^1/_2$ litre (1 pt) water per 500g (1lb) fruit. Heat on full power until liquid boils, and allow to cool. Then stir, and carry on cooking until fruit softens. Stand it. With tenderised dried fruit, cover with water and cook until almost tender. Allow to stand to finish cooking.

[CU] In general, there is no visible indication of degree of cooking, except for skins on fruit changing colour. It is usually a question of degree of softness when the fruit is tested with fork or finger. It is an easily learned skill.

Warning. Be very carefull when using full power on tiny amounts such as one small apple. The effect can be very vigorous. It may be better to use lower power and wait longer.

Pears in Red Wine

This is a classic example of poaching fruit. For a really good colour, use a cheap red wine.

Serves 4 Use 1 litre (2pint) casserole.
Allow 25 mins plus standing until cold.

150ml (5 fl.oz) water
150ml (5 fl.oz) wine
juice of one orange
175g (6oz) soft brown sugar
1 cinnamon stick
4 Comice pears, peeled and with stalks.

In the dish, combine the water, wine, orange juice and sugar.
Heat on medium/high until sugar is dissolved, stirring frequently. Bring to the boil on full power, and add cinnamon stick, and pears standing upright. Cook on medium/high until pears are tender. Stand until cold, then remove cinnamon.
Serve decorated with cream and orange slices.

Gooseberry Fool

Another popular sweet which is so easy by microwave.

Serves 4   Use 1 litre (2pint) deep casserole.
Allow 20mins. plus standing until cold.

500g (1lb) gooseberries, fresh or frozen.
Caster sugar to taste
Juice and grated rind of two oranges
275 ml (10 fl.oz) carton whipping cream
Chopped walnuts to garnish

Put the gooseberries in the dish, and if they are fresh, add water to moisten. Cover and cook on full power until soft. Then sieve or blend, and put back in the dish with the sugar. Heat on medium/high, stirring frequently until the sugar is dissolved. Add the orange and leave until cool.

Whip the cream until it is stiff, fold in the fruit, and then transfer to serving glasses. Decorate with nuts.

FISH

This can always be a success, with full flavour and unspoiled delicate texture. In fact, microwave cooks it superbly. Use full power except for single portions, reheating or for other seafoods.

Freshness is paramount. Clean fish well, and if it has a skin, smear the dish with melted butter to prevent it sticking. Arrange whole fish, such as trout, head to tail. Avoid thin areas by overlapping fillets, or folding tail under body. Cook brushed with melted fat, or add a little milk, wine, or stock. Always cover.

[CU] Fish should just begin to flake in the thinner parts. Thicker areas, partiularly round the bone, should still be slightly raw.
Be sure to accept this, cooking will be completed on standing.
Keep the cover on during standing time.

Fish

Trout with Almonds

Serves 4   Use a shallow dish
Allow 15 mins plus 5 mins standing.

50g (2oz) butter
50g (2oz) flaked almonds
four 200g (7 oz) trout
juice of one lemon
90ml (3fl.ozs) double cream
chopped parsley

Use full power to melt the butter in the dish, then add the almonds and cook until golden brown, stirring frequently.

Set the almonds aside. Arrange the trout in the dish, coating them with the butter remaining, and then sprinkle on the lemon juice. Cook covered, on full power.

[CU] the flesh of the fish flakes. Pour the cream over, and then use full power for just long enough to heat the cream. Allow to stand with cover on until the fish is perfect.

Serve sprinkled with the almonds and parsley.

Pasta and rice

Wight Shark Curry

Serves 4   Use 1.4 litre (2 ½ pint) casserole, small shallow dish

60g (2 ½ oz) desiccated coconut
small onion, finely chopped
2 tomatoes, finely chopped
25g (1oz) creamed coconut
75g (3ozs) frozen peas
1 tsp ground ginger
1 small green chilli, seeds removed, finely chopped
1 tbsp oil
1 tsp fenugreek seeds
2 tsp ground coriander
2 tbsp lemon juice
500g (1lb) shark or other meaty fish, cubed
lemon slices to garnish

Mix desiccated coconut with 300ml (½ pint) water. Warm using full power, then stand until cold. Drain off the milk and retain the pulp. Mix the milk with the onion, tomatoes, creamed coconut, peas, ginger and chilli. Cover, and heat on full power until boiling. Simmer at around medium power until onion is soft.

In shallow dish, combine oil, fenugreek and coriander. Heat at full power until fenugreek is just turning golden, and blend in coconut pulp. Add lemon juice and a little of the milk to make a smooth paste. Add the shark, cover, and cook on medium power, stirring often.
[CU] The fish just turning white.

Combine both mixtures, bring to the boil on full power, and then simmer on lower power for a few minutes, to combine flavours and textures.

PASTA AND RICE

Microwave is popular for these foods even though there is no great time saving. It's so convenient, and it doesn't steam up the kitchen. It is superb at re-heating them too. The high volume of water very nearly eliminates the usual microwave food characteristics, so it almost means using conventional packet instructions, including timings.

Choose a dish to suit your pasta type. For example, a long shallow dish for spaghetti. You might as well boil the water conventionally, using kettle or saucepan. That's better than microwave for large quantities.

Pasta and rice

Your container must be deep enough to allow for boiling up. Boiling over will be less likely if you add a tablespoon of oil. Having stirred in the pasta, make sure it is well covered with water, to prevent exposed parts dehydrating. Remember to stir once the water is boiling, to ensure that the pasta is well separated. After the final stir, put the cover back, and allow cooking to finish before you drain off the water.

[CU] This is almost inapplicable. Just test for tenderness.

Macaroni Cheese

The red Leicester cheese adds colour, but you can use others.
If you wish, you can add chopped ham, tomatoes, canned artichoke bottoms or prawns.

Serves 4-5   Use 2.75 ltr (5 pt) casserole and shallow serving dish
Allow 30 mins plus 10 mins standing

250g (8oz) uncooked macaroni
1.8 ltr (3 pints) boiling water
175g (6ozs) Red Leicester cheese, grated
2 size three eggs, beaten
300ml ($1/_2$ pint) milk
1 tsp made mustard, strong
1 pkt crisps, crushed
Salt and pepper

Put the macaroni in the dish with the water and a little salt.
Cover and cook on full power until almost tender. Drain off the liquid and stir in the cheese, eggs, milk and mustard.
Heat uncovered until the mixture begins to thicken around the edges. Continue heating and stirring until it is piping hot throughout. Pour into serving dish and sprinkle with crisps.

Pasta and rice

Vegetable Lasagne

A real family favourite, filling and full of flavour. You can choose alternative vegetables to suit yourself. This recipe uses the "no need to pre-cook" type of lasagne.

Serves 4-5   Use 1.1 litre (2pint) bowl; shallow serving dish. Allow 30mins.

1 onion, chopped
275g (10oz) courgettes, sliced
275g (10oz) carrots, peeled and thinly sliced
1 red pepper, seeded and thinly sliced
half a vegetable stock cube
150ml (5 fl.ozs) cold water
600ml (1 pint) thick white sauce
12 sheets lasagne
175g (6oz) grated Cheddar cheese

Put the onion, courgettes, carrots and pepper into the bowl with the stock cube and water. Cover, and heat on full power until the water is very hot, and the stock cube begins to dissolve. Stir well and continue cooking until the vegetables are just tender. Drain the liquor from the vegetables and add it to the sauce, stirring well. Pour a thin layer of the sauce into the serving dish, cover it with pasta, then a layer of vegetables, and top that with cheese. Add further layers to use up the ingredients, and finish with cheese on top of sauce. Cook until the lasagne is tender. Use full power, but reduce it to control any overflowing. Stand food for five minutes.

RICE

Basically, there are two ways of cooking rice. One is to use more water than it can absorb and then drain off what is left.
This needs about 750 ml ($1^{1}/_{4}$ pints) of water per 250g (8oz) of rice. Use boiling water. This method is best for brown rice.

The other method is to estimate a precise amount of water so that it is all absorbed by the rice. That needs experience. As there are now so many types of rice, neither method will always be better than the other. Here are some pointers:

Preferably, first rinse the rice to wash away surplus starch.
Times on rice packages can generally be reduced by a quarter. Always use boiling water, a deep container (not too heavy), and a cover. Stir occasionally, and stop the energy when the rice is still firm. With the

absorption method, stop while the rice is still quite wet and sloppy, and if the grains are still too hard, add a bit more boiling water and continue. Allow plenty of standing time and it will work like magic. Never be tempted to carry on cooking until the rice appears to be just right for serving. If you do it will finish up like a brick.

Green Rice

This shows how stock and vegetables can add flavour and colour.
Serves 4   Use 1.75 litre (3 pint) casserole
Allow 20 mins plus 5 mins standing.

2 green peppers, de-seeded and chopped
one small onion, quartered
50g (2oz) chopped parsley
175g (6oz) long grain rice
400ml (14 fl.ozs) boiling water
Seasoning

Using a blender or processor, blend peppers, onion and parsley until smooth. Put everything into the dish and cook on full power, stirring several times, until rice is just tender. Drain off any surplus liquor. Allow to stand.

POULTRY

The first essential is to have poultry at an even temperature throughout when you start cooking it. For a succulent result it must be carefully cooked. A whole bird should be cooked breast side down on a roasting rack, lightly coated with fat, and with a loose cover such as a roasting bag, slit for part ventilation.

Cook for half your rough estimate time, then turn it over and continue until the juices run clear.

[CU] Test by piercing between leg and carcass - on both sides. It should be only just cooked. Resist the temptation to cook longer, you'll make it tough and stringy.

Poultry

Give up to half an hour of standing time, that will finish off the cooking so that the meat feels relaxed under the skin. Use a similar technique for joints and portions, remembering to arrange them with thinner parts to the centre. They will not need so much standing.

Microwave cooks poultry superbly, but it is not good at browning it. An attractive finish can be achieved by using a marinade, or by brushing on seasonings as in the next recipe.

Tandoori Turkey

Serves 4   Use roasting rack
Allow 15 mins. Stand 10-15 mins

4 turkey drumsticks
300ml (½ pint) natural yogurt
1 tsp salt
juice of one lemon
good pinch chilli powder
1 tbsp paprika
2 tsp ground ginger
1 tbsp tomato puree

Make several deep slits in the flesh of the turkey drumsticks.
Combine all remaining ingredients, and use this mixture as a marinade for the drumsticks overnight in the refrigerator.

Arrange the drumsticks on the roasting rack, and cook them on full power. [CU] the juices run clear. Cover loosely with aluminium foil and stand to soften for 5-10 mins.

Chicken with asparagus

Serves 4   Use 1.5 litre (2½ pint) deep casserole
Allow 20 mins.

25g (1oz) butter
1 onion, finely chopped
1 stick celery, finely chopped
25g (1oz) flour
400g (14 oz) can asparagus tips
150ml (¾ pint) dry white wine
100g (4oz) button mushrooms, sliced
350g (12ozs) cooked chicken, cut into pieces
salt and pepper
90ml (3 fl. ozs) cream

Put butter, onion and celery into casserole. Cover, and cook until vegetables are tender. Sprinkle on the flour, cook on medium power until slightly bubbly. Stir well. Blend in the strained asparagus liquid and the wine. Bring to the boil, stirring whenever it thickens around the edges. Add asparagus, mushrooms, and chicken. Cook, covered, on medium high until chicken is well heated through and mushrooms cooked. Stir in the cream and heat long enough to recover temperature. Serve sprinkled with toasted breadcrumbs.

SAUCES

Sauces and toppings, savoury or sweet, are very quick and easy by microwave. As there is no external heat, you can have lump-free results without the chore of continuous stirring.

Start with all ingredients to hand, and use a jug or bowl with a curved base, and a good handle to grip as you beat the sauce. For a really smooth sauce, use a small whisk and make sure it touches the bottom of the bowl. Sauces do need care and attention, so don't wander off.

If your roux is made with flour, cook it for several seconds before adding the liquid, otherwise it will taste raw. When using a thickening agent, stir as soon as the sauce begins to thicken round the edges, whisk well and carry on cooking.

[CU] Having proceeded as above, watch for the sauce to rise. As soon as it does, whisk it, and it's finished. The same thing goes for packet gravies and custards.

Sauces

Here is a simple sauce to practice with.

White Sauce

Serves 4   Use 1 litre (1³/₄ pint) jug
Allow 6 mins.

25g (1oz) butter
25g (1oz) plain flour
300ml (¹/₂ pint) milk
salt and pepper

Use full power. Melt the butter in the jug, stir in the flour, and cook until it is crumbly and slightly bubbly. That should take less than a minute.

Gradually whisk in the milk. Then heat until the mixture begins to thicken at the edges. Stir well, and then heat until it all thickens, leading up to [CU]. That takes a few minutes. Whisk, and season to taste. Now you can add cheese, ham, parsley or anything you fancy.

With a sweet sauce of this type, cook it without the sugar. You can store it that way too. Then if you stir in the sugar just before serving, you'll not get a skin forming on top.

Chocolate Sauce

Serves 8   Use 1 litre (1³/₄ pint) jug
Allow 6 mins.

150ml (¹/₄ pint) milk
2 tbsp cocoa powder
1 tbsp cornflour
250g (8 oz) light soft brown sugar
2 tbsp golden syrup
pinch of salt
knob of butter

Mix cocoa, cornflour and sugar to a smooth paste with a little milk. Blend in the remaining milk, syrup and salt. Heat on full power. Stir when it begins to thicken around the edges, heat again, and stir when it reaches [CU]. Then stir in butter.

At the beginning, the cocoa powder is much easier to blend in if a little hot milk is used instead of cold.

Scrambled Eggs

Serves 2   Use 600ml (1 pint) jug

3 tbsp milk
15g (½oz) butter
4 eggs size two
salt and pepper

Beat together all ingredients in the jug. Using full power, cook until mixture begins to rise and thicken around the edges. Stir gently, thoroughly dispersing the cooked parts.
Do the same again, until [CU] is reached.

[CU] The eggs should have the texture of wallpaper paste.

Allow to stand. The longer the standing, the dryer the end product.

For a single egg, use a straight sided cup, and a fork.
Watch very carefully. Stir and break up well when half cooked.

[CU] Catch it as it rises nearly to the top of the cup, and stir briskly for
    half a minute.

MEAT

You'll never enjoy a succulent joint from a poor piece of meat. The first essential is to go to a good butcher. If you have doubts about your meat, learn about marinades for tenderising.

Choose a joint with a good cylindrical shape. If that's not what you want, then shield the thinner parts with foil, as described on page 48. Cook the joint on a roasting rack, and cover it with a roasting dome or a loose, slit roasting bag. Never put the joint in the bag. The slit allows steam to escape, leaving a jacket of hot air around the joint.

First use full power for two minutes per half kg (1lb) of meat. That simply raises its temperature to the point where it begins to cook. For joints larger than 1.5 kg. (3lb), use your oven's cookbook as a guide to cooking time, but remember to make your checks well before the full time is up.

If your book suggests the same power level for all weights, with a minutes per pound chart, then you must work differently for joints smaller than 1.5kg (3lb). So reduce the power roughly in proportion to the weight, but

Meat

not to less than medium/low or de-frost power. That will increase the cooking time, which is the whole idea of it. The meat will then brown better and eat better. Cook even more slowly if you wish.

> [CU] After long deliberation, we have concluded that the use of a thermometer is essential if you are to cook a joint to your liking first time, and consistently so from then on. Any good meat thermometer will do if you are not going to put it in the oven. If it is to go in with the meat, you must have one designed for microwave use. The joint will be ready for its standing time when the temperature at its centre is as follows:
>
> | | | |
> |---|---|---|
> | BEEF | Rare | 55°C/130°F |
> | BEEF | Medium | 63°C/145°F |
> | BEEF | Well done | 70°C/160°F |
> | LAMB | Pink | 60°C/140°F |
> | LAMB | Well done | 70°C/160°F |
> | PORK | Always well done | 80°C/175°F |
>
> The joint must now stand, covered, for at least as long as it has already been cooking. Not until that time is up, will it be cooked as required. Do not carve it before then.

With chops, burgers etc. you may prefer to use a browning dish. Whichever way you cook those, if the juices run clear, they are done; but always avoid giving extra time to make sure. That could ruin them.

For casseroles, choose a tender cut of meat, and use full power until boiling, then reduce the level to whatever will simmer the food, first try half power.

Beef mince should be made to take at least half the conventional recipe time, and stewing steak two thirds. Force it to cook faster, by using too high a power level, and it will be tough.

Meat

Chilli con carne

Serves 4-6   Use 1.75 litre (3 pt) casserole
Allow 40 mins. plus 10 mins. standing

1 tbsp oil
2 onions, chopped
1 green pepper, chopped
500g (1lb) minced beef
Chilli powder to taste
400g (14 oz) can chopped tomatoes
425g (15oz) can red kidney beans, drained
Salt

Combine the oil, onions and green pepper in the dish. Cook on full power, without a cover, until the onion is opaque. Stir several times.

Add the mince and cook until it changes colour, stirring often. Add the rest of the ingredients, and continue at full power until boiling.

Reduce power to med/high and carry on until meat is cooked and flavours have mingled.   Allow it to settle for ten minutes before serving.

Kebabs

The microwave oven is very good at cooking these. Use wooden skewers.

Serves 4   Use roasting rack and 1.1 litre (2 pint) bowl.
Allow 15 mins.

Marinade

150ml (5fl.ozs) red wine
2 tbsp oil
2 tbsp mango chutney
2 tbsp brown sugar
1 tbsp curry powder

Other ingredients

2 eating apples, cored and cubed
8 button mushrooms
8 slices of a small lemon

Continued over

KEBAB METHOD
Combine the marinade ingredients in the bowl, and heat on medium high power until the sugar has dissolved.
Stir in the meat and leave for two hours.

Drain meat and thread onto skewers together with apple, mushrooms and lemon. Using full power, cook on roasting rack.

[CU] Meat juices run clear and meat is fairly soft when squeezed.

Brush with marinade during cooking. Allow to stand, covered, for several minutes, to even out temperature.

PUDDINGS
Everyone loves a pudding, and the microwave oven produces them in no time at all, even those traditional slow cooking puds.

Cook your first sponge pudding without a cover, so that you can watch it. Keep an eye on its glistening wet surface.
The pudding will soon rise, and then heave up and down.

> [CU] Watch the area of sticky surface become smaller and smaller, until it is confined to the edges or centre. BEFORE the last trace can disappear, OPEN THE DOOR. The pudding should then sink just a little. If it sinks low in the basin, cook a bit longer.

Wait a minute or two, (not just a second or two) and plunge a knife down to the bottom, to check that it is cooked right through. If it is not, cook a little more. When all is well, be sure to stand the pudding for at least five minutes, and up to twenty. That will enhance both flavour and texture.

The above method is very easy indeed, but you must have it clear in your mind. It is no good trying to follow the book as you go through the motions. The pudding may overtake you.

When you become used to how long it takes, you will have established your timing. Most puddings cook well without a cover, but if you do use one, it will shorten the time.

Puddings

Crumbles

The microwave oven is ideal for crumble toppings, but do not overcook in an attempt to make them change colour. They will not. For varying the colour and texture, use combinations of cereals, nuts, sugars and flours.

[CU] The only test is to sample the topping for a cooked flavour, and the fruit to see whether that is right too.

Flan Cases

Flan cases made from pastry can be very successfully cooked by microwave. The colour will be pale, but the taste and texture can be excellent. Use either plain flour, or a mixture of plain and wholemeal.

[CU] The pastry will dry and become a paler colour as it cooks. You must learn, by experience, to recognise this condition.

Puddings

Here's the perfect example of a look and see recipe:

Creme Caramel

Serves 6   Use 1.4 litre (2½ pint) Pyrex bowl
             6 small ramekins
             600ml (1 pint) jug

Allow 30mins, then stand until cold.

150ml (5 fl. ozs) water
150g (5 ozs) caster sugar
425ml (¾ pint) gold top milk
3 number two eggs

Using medium power, heat 100g (4 ozs) of sugar in the bowl with the water, stirring once or twice until dissolved. Using full power, boil it until it becomes golden brown. Pour the resulting syrup into the ramekins.

Warm the milk. Whisk the eggs with the remaining sugar, and stir into the warmed milk. Pour this mixture, through a sieve, onto the caramel in the ramekins, and cook on medium power.

[CU] Mixture only just set.

Have them arranged in a circle wih a loose cover. Allow to stand, covered, until cold. For a perfect finish, you may need to turn the ramekins during cooking.

Puddings

Fruit Crumble

Serves 4-5   Use 1.2 litre (2 pint) shallow dish
Allow 15 mins.

750g (1½ lb) prepared fruit
100g (4oz) soft brown sugar
100g (4oz) butter
175g (6oz) plain flour
50g (2oz) demerara sugar
25g (1oz) chopped walnuts

Mix the fruit with the sugar and arrange it evenly in the dish. Rub the butter with the flour and combine this with the other dry ingredients. Sprinkle that over the fruit. Cook on full power.

[CU] Fruit almost softened, and topping tasting cooked.

Allow to stand, to even out the temperature.

Traditional Sponge Pudding

Serves 4   Use 1.2 litre (2 pint) pudding basin
Allow 5 mins plus 5 mins minimum standing.

100g (4oz) soft margarine
100g (4oz) self raising flour
100g (4oz) caster sugar
1 tbsp milk
2 eggs, size two
Jam

Lightly grease the mixing bowl. Mix together all the ingredients except the jam. Mix well. Pour into the bowl and cover lightly. Cook on full power.

[CU] See earlier full description.

Stand at least five minutes, and on turning it out of the basin, pour over some heated jam. Remember that small amounts of jam heat very quickly indeed. Work in seconds, not minutes.

CAKES AND BAKES

A larger number of disastrous cakes have been produced by microwave than by any other means of cooking. This has been caused not only by overcooking, but by overmixing.

> The golden rule is: mix thoroughly the fat and sugar with the eggs, but when it comes to the flour, gently fold it in.

Microwave cooking is not going to brown these foods very much, but their appearance can be enhanced by the use of the darker sugars and yellower fats.

Cakes

Once a cake mix is in its cooking container, level off the surface and then make a slight well in the centre. Stand the container on a plastic rack, not directly on the oven tray or base, and cover with a piece of absorbant kitchen paper.

[CU] The surface of the cake will be just dry, and the centre will have risen to become almost level. Test by inserting a thin knife deep down at the centre. Allow adequate standing time before turning the cake out.

Biscuits

Cook these six at a time. Arrange in a circle on a sheet of non-stick baking parchment. They will cook very quickly. As the surface upon which they stand becomes progressively hotter, each load will cook even faster than the previous one.

[CU] Biscuits change colour as they cook. They take on a dryer appearance and will be cooked sufficiently when the "puffing" subsides.

Remove carefully from the oven, as the edges can still be soft. Leave on a cooling rack until done.

TRAY BAKES, flapjacks etc..

[CU] Stop cooking when the mixture begins to bubble all over. With less fatty mixtures, such as shortbread, stop cooking when a small circle is left slightly raw in the centre.

Cakes and bakes

Golden Flapjacks

Makes 8   Use 2 litre (3$^{1}/_{2}$ pint) jug, 20cm (8inch) flan dish. Allow 8 mins. Stand until cold.

3 tbsp golden syrup
75g (3 ozs) butter
65g (2 $^{1}/_{2}$ ozs) soft brown sugar
175g (6 ozs) rolled oats
75g (3 ozs) mixed chopped walnuts and glace cherries

Using medium power, heat the syrup, butter and sugar in the jug until melted. Combine all ingredients, and stir well.

Turn the mixture into the flan dish and spread it out evenly. Cook, uncovered, on full power.

[CU] The mixture has just begun to bubble all over.

Mark into eight wedges, and leave until cold before cutting.

Menu planning

At this stage, you are able to cook basic foods and recipes, and now you want to put together suitable combinations to make up complete meals. You will, of course, have heeded the warning given earlier about being too ambitious with your first attempt at a meal. Here, then, are some carefully laid out meal plans which run smoothly. Menus are for four people.

Whole chicken
New potatoes
Carrots with peas
Gravy   Blackberry and apple crumble

Allow one and a half hours.

Cook fruit for crumble and make up topping, cover fruit with topping. This dish can be cooked first, or as the table is being cleared after the first course.

Make up gravy. Juices from meat, and vegetable water can be added later. Prepare vegetables. These are presumed to be fresh potatoes and carrots with frozen peas.

Cook chicken to [CU] and leave to stand. Cook potatoes to [CU], drain and leave to stand. Cook carrots to half way, add peas and continue to [CU]. Add juices etc. to gravy, stir and re-heat.

Kebabs
Chinese vegetables
White rice   Sponge pudding

Allow fifty minutes.

The pudding and rice will stay hot equally well, and for a very long time. If it does become necesssary, rice re-heats better, and so the recommended order of cooking is;
rice, pudding, vegetables and kebabs last. Heat jam for pudding just before serving it.

Menu planning

Soup
Trout with almonds
Green rice
Baked tomatoes
Pears in red wine

Allow eighty minutes, or sixty minutes if pears are done in advance.

It is presumed that the soup has been made previously. The trout and the rice stay hot equally well, but it is better for the rice to precede the trout, in case it should cool.

Use this sequence; pears, rice, and then trout. Do the tomatoes when the soup is at the table. Just halve them, dot with butter and heat through. If necesssary, re-heat rice while you clear the soup dishes.

A VERY SUBSTANTIAL MEAL

Chilli con carne
Jacket potatoes
Green beans
Creme caramel

Allow seventy minutes, or longer if the creme caramel is not prepared in advance. The jacket potatoes could go first, but the chilli is enhanced by a final brief re-heat.

Work in this order:

Creme caramel well in advance, chilli, potatoes, beans.
If necessary, and preferably, boost the chilli before serving.

USING MICROWAVE TOGETHER WITH CONVENTIONAL EQUIPMENT

There's no reason for microwave to be a loner. For even greater ease and versatility, use it in conjuncion with a kettle when boiling water is needed in volume. Use microwave to blanch potatoes for chips or conventional roasting. "Flash" small meat items under the grill before cooking by microwave, and brown microwave rice puddings under the grill before serving. There will always be foods which are better done conventionally, just as there are many which are better done by microwave. Strike the right balance and enjoy all that traditional and microwave methods have to offer.

A BRIGHT FUTURE FOR YOU AND FOR MICROWAVE

We hope you have enjoyed the experience of re-shaping your idea of microwave ovens and food. Over the years, microwave has had its ups and downs, and we think you will now agree with us that the downs have been totally unjustified, and all a matter of misconceptions, misunderstandings and misinformation.

To us, microwave is easy to understand and easy to use, and we have done our best to make it that way for everyone who reads this book.

Some people will have found it childishly simple, others will not. That is the way of things. Do not expect to become an expert just by reading the book. Almost everything which has been covered can become second nature to you, providing you practice it long enough to get it into your system.

Please go on to read about looking after your microwave oven. Don't leave it until something goes wrong. Why not take a look at the Small Print too? As small print goes, it is very unusual in that it reveals things instead of hiding them.

We would like to thank you for the time you have spent with the book, and wish you every success with your microwave work.

Looking after your oven

Two things are really bad for microwave ovens. Running them empty, and putting metal objects inside them. Bear this in mind always, and take all necessary precautions.

Microwave ovens do not have hot surfaces, so they need no more than a mild detergent to keep them clean. They do not work properly when they are dirty. Abrasive cloths and cleaners spoil the surface of stainless steel and plastics. Solvents can also ruin plastics. Combination ovens are more trouble to clean, because they do have hot surfaces, and food spatterings can bake onto them. With those, you may have to resort to oven cleaner. Use the brush-on type. You'll be better able to control where it goes. Identify any self-cleaning panels before you start. Be careful with the small "waveguide cover" which the oven may have at the top or side of the cavity. It can look almost like a label, and it can be fragile. If you damage it, it will have to be replaced. With a combination oven, you can turn on the heat to dry it off, but make doubly sure it's on convection, and not microwave or combination.

SO YOU THINK YOUR OVEN IS FAULTY !
Microwave ovens are pretty reliable, but they can fail at any time just like any other electrical appliance. Even if that happens during the first week, it doesn't mean you have a bad oven, simply one with a fault, and probably a very minor fault. Never take the oven apart or try to do your own repairs, or carry on in the hope that it will get better. Trivial faults can lead to serious problems. If you suspect a fault, speak to a qualified engineer and preferably one who is authorised by the oven manufacturer. Before you do that, make sure you are not mistaken, and where appropriate, check the simple things you may be able to correct. Here are some troubles which could crop up. They are not all real faults.

DISHES GETTING HOT
A dish cannot always stay cool in a microwave oven. One which is full of boiling food may have to be handled with a cloth. Consider what is in a dish and how long it has been heating, and common sense will tell you whether it's likely to be hot. Dishes do need to be sparkling clean. Even a faint dull film on the surface can absorb energy and generate heat. The same goes for oven trays. Quite strong detergents are sometimes needed to get them really clean.

Dishes are sometimes made of materials which absorb a lot of microwave energy, and they can reach searing temperatures. Nothing can be done about it, just stop using them in the microwave oven. Old glass ovenware with a spoiled surface can also absorb energy. To test a utensil (non-metallic), put it in the oven with a separate half-cup of water. After heating on full power for about a minute, the item you are testing should be no more than slightly warm.

OVEN INTERIOR GETTING HOT
Again, this may not be abnormal. The interior can be quite hot after the oven has cooked a large quantity of food for a lengthy period. Soiled surfaces can heat, so the oven may need cleaning. If a part of the interior gets really hot after just a short while, have the oven checked by an engineer.

An oven running empty can get extremely hot, just as it can with a very light load such as popcorn. Don't use it repeatedly for anything like that. It is assumed that the oven is properly ventilated, with unobstructed air passages, and not up against anything hot.

OVEN LACKING POWER
This can be due to a fault or aging, but it is very often caused by a poor mains supply. If that is the problem, the oven may work normally some of the time. Check it with a cup of water at various times of day to see whether there is a variation in performance. If there is, it will almost certainly be the power at fault. The trouble can be confined to a socket or a room, or it can be the house or the entire district. If you suspect a supply problem, you could ask an electrician specifically to checked the voltage, or call out the microwave oven engineer, who should normally check power supply before looking for an oven fault.

PROBLEMS WITH DE-FROSTING
You can have a fault affecting only a switched de-frost power, but it is unlikely with variable power. Most de-frost "faults" are user misunderstandings. That shouldn't arise with anyone who has read this book.

Looking after your oven

TOUCH CONTROLS HAYWIRE
If wrong numbers are displayed or just parts of numbers, or if nothing happens when you touch the controls, it can be due to water having found its way around the control panel and into some sensitive area. Never attempt to take the oven to pieces to dry it out, that would be dangerous for you and for the oven. You can try one thing. Leave the oven in a warm room for a couple of days. That may cure the trouble completely. If it doesn't, call the engineer. Other problems are possible with touch controls, and faults which lie elsewhere can put them out of acion.

STEAM FROM AROUND THE OVEN DOOR
This is quite common and it doesn't show that there is anything wrong with the door seals. Microwave seals do not need to be airtight, steam tight or light tight, and nowadays, doors don't even need to fit tightly. Many doors are a close fit, and it is easier to make them that way than to deal with thousands of people wanting them altered because they think they are wrong. Microwaves are not carried by air or steam or light. Excessive air can be forced out around the door if the vents at the top or rear of the oven are blocked. Always see that vents are clear, and don't put things on top of the oven.
See the Small Print for a fuller explanation of oven doors.

TINGLE WHEN THE OVEN IS TOUCHED
This won't be the microwaves. It will be an earthing problem. You can get it with any appliance made of metal - if the electrical earthing is defective. Look inside the plug, see that the wires are in the right places, and the screws are tight. Don't run it through an adapter. If you still have trouble, the electrician is the first person to consult.

OVEN ABSOLUTELY "DEAD"
First check that it is switched on. Then check that something else will work in its socket.

If it has overheated, try it again after an hour, and without changing its fuse. That way you'll avoid fitting a dud one or the wrong type. Some models work again when they have cooled down - but others do not. If it does work again, SOUNDING NORMAL, and there is no external reason for the overheating, give it a good test, making sure it has proper ventilation, and call an engineer if you have further trouble. If it had not overheated, check the plug wiring and fuse. Virtually all microwave ovens should have a thirteen amp fuse in the plug, but it is not likely to blow. There is usually a more sensitive fuse inside the oven. That will be a special type which is not accessible to the owner. In any case, checks have to be made to find the reason for its failure.

Looking after your oven

SPARKS OR BURNING INSIDE THE OVEN
Where something in the cavity (where the food goes) has ignited, it is usually because the oven has run empty. It may have had something inside it to begin with, but over an excessive period it has evaporated or burned away. That would have caused the energy to concentrate on food spatterings in the nooks and crannies. Sometimes, the remains of food will burn and set fire to something else. If this has happened, call the engineer.

Sparks and violent snapping sounds can be caused by small pices of metal foil on foodstuffs or packaging. Although this is very alarming, it is not likely to cause immediate damage to the oven. If this is your trouble, remove the offending object, clean and test the oven as for the burned food problem.

When food has been destroyed in a microwave oven, things are usually not as bad as they seem to be, so first clean the interior thoroughly and wipe it dry. Have a good look at every part of it, and if it all appears to be in perfect condition, with not the smallest trace of burning, heat a cup of water, and on no account start the oven without it.

Watch carefully, and open the door if there is any visual sign of trouble. Very probably, the oven will not have suffered in the slightest, and everything will be normal except for a very strange burning smell - like an electrical burn-out. Do not be deceived by this. Providing the oven does work properly, all you have to do is put up with that smell for a few days or even weeks. It is caused by deposits from the destroyed food which have found their way into inaccessible places, and it will die away eventually. You could call an engineer to dismantle the oven and clean the air passages but even that may not completely cure the smell, although, of course, it may be better for your peace of mind.

SERVICING
This is not the same as simple leakage testing, although a service would include a leakage test. In short, servicing entails dismantling the oven to check that it is working properly, and taking certain actions to ensure that it has the best chance of carrying on that way. For most home models, this attention is not required more often than every three or four years. It is different if the oven has very heavy use or if it is in a greasy or dusty atmosphere. In extreme cases, annual servicing may be necessary. See the Small Print for more detailed information.

LEAKAGE TESTING

This is not needed at any specific intervals. It depends on how much the oven is used. Top manufacturers find negligible leakage on samples of their production line ovens, even after the doors have been opened and closed one hundred thousand times. Do not buy a test-it-yourself meter unless you are prepared to pay the high price of a professional model. That is unnecessary, and cheap meters are quite useless.

> There is no evidence that anyone has ever been harmed by energy leakage from a microwave oven. That's in forty years, and enough to convince almost anyone. Statistics, if they exist, would probably show that no cooker has a better safety record.

OVEN LAMPS

These can fail at any time, just like other lamps. The oven usually carries on working, but when a lamp breaks down, it can blow the oven's internal fuse, then it will go dead. The fuse may blow weeks after the lamp fails, so replace lamps promptly. Don't try to do it yourself if it means removing the cabinet. At the moment, most ovens do have to be taken apart for lamp replacements, and that must be done only by a qualified person.

You can do two things to improve the life expectancy of your oven lamp. Keep the top of the oven clear and well ventilated, and avoid slamming the door particularly if it is the drop down type. Lamps are sensitive to vibration, especially old lamps. Should the lamp fail and then work again, have that investigated, A blown fuse might be the next thing.

MISCELLANEOUS FAULTS

There are dozens of potential failure points in any microwave oven - and with electronic controls there are thousands - though most are microscopic and would fit on a pin head. With micro electronics, it can take little to halt the operation of a microwave oven.

Though they may not seem to justify it, minor malfunctions should be investigated. Try to provide the engineer with accurate information about the circumstances in which a fault became apparent. If the oven stopped working altogether, it will help if you know what was happening when it stopped. Was it in the middle of doing something, or did it simply not work when you came to use it? Did it go pop soon after you pressed the start button, or as you opened the door? With an oven which is "dead", this information is very helpful to a service engineer who finds everything in order - apart from a blown fuse.

Looking after your oven

For moving house, the oven is best transported in its original packing. Never lift the oven by its door or handle. That might cause it not to work. Trays and suchlike should never be transported inside the oven unless they are suitably cushioned. Tape the door to the cabinet to prevent it rubbing up and down. Remember that most of the oven weight is probably at one end, so carry that end close to your body.

If you want to take your oven to another country, check that the mains voltage and frequency are right. A 240 volt oven may not work at all well on 220 volts, and it might stop heating the food altogether if that voltage drops a small percentage. Seek the advice of the oven manufacturer at the outset.

If you want to use your microwave oven on a portable generator, in boat or caravan for example, make no mistake about its consumption. Remember that it is double its wattage output. For a six hundred watt model you must allow 1.2kw. .

If you decide to take up catering, get a real catering model. You will probably do best with the most powerful one you can afford. As well as having extra power, commercial microwave ovens will stand up to heavy use, and a fair amount of abuse. Don't expect to get many frills and refinements. They are not necessary. A commercial oven is essentially simple, solid and reliable. Make enquiries about the service provided by the intended supplier. Even if the model you are buying has a good reputation for reliability, you may join the unlucky few who do have trouble with one.

The small print

DE-FROSTING

Most old microwave ovens had only high power. The de-frosting procedure with those, was to stop the oven every few minutes to rest the food. Few caterers ever complained about this tedius process, but when it came to home users it was a different matter. This brought about the low power called de-frost, and the "de-frost switch" soon became a sought-after feature. If it had simply been called low power, it might have been more widely used. Fewer people would have regarded it as a magic de-froster which should be incapable of cooking or heating.

There are basically two ways of providing reduced power. Power can be interrupted, as it usually is with hotplates, or the oven can be made to generate a continuous low power. Some models used one system and some the other, and they both worked satisfactorily. The intermittent system is easier and probably cheaper for the manufacturer. It predominated, and it gave demonstrators more to talk about. Their sales patter gained the terms "pulsing" and "de-frost cycle" and they spoke of ice particles "breaking down" and dispersing during the "rest" part of the cycle.

That is one way of describing what happens, but it can be argued that continuous low power also has advantages. It provides a gentle and gradual process, without repeated heating and cooling. It can never subject the food to a high energy level. No doubt the systems have different effects somewhere, and on balance, continuous power is possibly marginally better. This is sometimes disputed. It has so far not been found practicable to have more than three powers without using the intermittent system, so nowadays, with variable power, all levels except full can be said to "pulse". They all cycle on and off. Continuous de-frost power is still used, but mainly on commercial models.

AUTO DE-FROST was devised to enable a pre-set oven to cook or re-heat immediately following the de-frost stage, and without the need for the intervening standing time. The system is not suitable for all types of frozen food, and manufacturers' advice should be followed. Auto de-frost usually divides the set time into three equal periods; at medium power, low power and then very low power. If six minutes is set, it will provide two minutes at each power. The total period roughly equals normal de-frost time plus standing time. Caution is advised when setting up such a sequence for an unattended oven. With no one to watch, there is no certainty that the food will be properly de-frosted before it is re-heated. It is best to rehearse the meal procedure at a time when it can be checked.

VARIABLE POWER ACTION

Variable power is usually high power "thinned out" by being interrupted every few seconds. Here is an explanation of how it is usually done, and the peculiarities of a typical system. Not all systems are exactly like this.

The transmitter device is the magnetron, which has a glowing filament heated by a low voltage. It also uses a very high voltage to produce the microwave energy. About every thirty seconds, the power control switches off both voltages, stopping the energy output. The energy is delayed for two seconds at the start of each cycle, while the magnetron warms up. Half power then, is energy on for fifteen seconds and off for fifteen seconds, repeatedly. Other powers are proportional.

Suppose half power is selected, and the oven is set to run for only fifteen seconds, it can be the fifteen seconds of full power - half of the thirty second cycle. It will still be the same if the oven runs for up to thirty seconds. Anyone selecting say twenty seconds at half power, would hardly expect to get fifteen at full power, but that's how it can be. Forty five seconds running time gives three 15 second half cycles, two on and one off, making 30 seconds on and 15 seconds off - and that is still not half power. This assumes that the cycle starts at the beginning, with the energy coming on, but that is not always the case.

ELECTRONIC VERSUS MECHANICAL

Electronic controls always start the cycle at the beginning. Mechanical controls usually do not, they can start at any point in the cycle, quite by chance. They have a cam mechanism which carries on rotating even when full power is selected.

With those, fifteen seconds at half power, could be the on half of the thirty second cycle, the off half, or a bit of each, depending on how far round the rotating cam happened to be when the start button was pressed. The oven might produce full power, or no power, or anything in between.

The small print

De-frost level gives a cycle of about ten seconds on and twenty off. Thirty seconds of de-frost power (one full cycle) is actually ten seconds of full power. That is how it will be with electronics, but with mechanical controls, the ten seconds of energy could start at any time during the thirty seconds. So it could if the oven runs for only twenty seconds. With the cycle not starting at the beginning, what actually happens is pure chance, and if the oven is set for a very short time, there could be absolutely no effect on the food. This may take some thinking over but it is fact, and it does make perfect sense. In practice, these very short times are rarely used, so it doesn't often matter.

These inaccuracies are the reason for advising a minimum of one minute for the use of reduced power. As you can see, there is little point in using it for shorter periods. You might just as well use full power and be certain of what is happening. Now that you know about these peculiarities, you can decide for yourself when to use variable power. For periods longer than one minute, the errors of the control are insignificant.

CAVITY DESIGN

The space inside a microwave oven is called its cavity, and its shape and size affect oven performance. It is all related to the length of the microwaves which are being reflected around inside, and the way they can converge and resonate to produce uneven heating of the load. The shape and position of the food itself can further affect heating patterns. Distribution devices continually alter the reflected paths of the microwave energy and/or the disances between the food and the cavity walls. Their object is to shift or cancel out uneven patterns. Turntable systems move the food through the uneven heating patterns. As smaller cavities tend to give faster results at a given wattage, it is perhaps best to have the smallest cavity which is capable of serving its purpose.

ACCURACY OF ELECTRONIC CONTROLS

Electronic timers are strongly favoured for their accuracy, and many of them can be set to the nearest second. It must be remembered, though, that oven time will be short by the two or three seconds the magnetron takes to warm up. Over very short periods, that rather spoils the accuracy. More important, is the "inaccuracy" of most foods, so the precision of the timer can be wasted. The exception could be something like a container with carefully measured contents, stored at a controlled temperature. As this book propounds, many things requiring short times and accurate heating are better done manually with no timing at all.

A solitary scrambled egg, for example, would need timing to within two or three seconds for anyone who is fussy but it's time is unpredictable. Typically, one egg takes a minute to scramble, but it could easily be anything between forty and eighty seconds, eggs vary enormously.

FOOD STAYING HOT

This phenomenon has been explained in several ways. It has been suggested that microwave food reaches an exceedingly high temperature and takes a long time to cool. That is not true. Then it is the heat taking time to find its way out from the centre of the mass or into the centre from the outside. The explanation you are offered here is the flywheel effect. All heat is movement of molecules. In a microwave oven, the molecules move in sympathy with the microwaves. They change direction nearly five thousand million times a second. That is so fast that they take a very long time to slow down. It is an adequate and understandable explanation, whether or not it is absolutely accurate.

OVEN INTERIORS

All microwave oven cavities have to be made of metal, because it is the only thing which is capable of containing the energy. Many owners think that their ovens have "plastic" interiors. What they see is a painted coating on the surface of the metal. Stainless steel interiors are favoured in the U.K. and they are certainly very durable and rust free. An acrylic painted interior from a reliable manufacturer can be perfectly satisfactory as long as it is treated with care.

METAL IN MICROWAVE OVENS

The best advice to give any microwave user is never to put metal of any kind inside the oven - while it is working. The oven itself has to be metal, and so we are talking about additional metallic objects which are unattached to the earthed interior. Instructions have already been given about the use of aluminium foil, and they must be strictly observed. If foil does come near the cavity wall, arcing may result, because it will have developed a high voltage in relation to the cavity. Arcing can burn a hole right through the wall. The voltage does not matter as long as the "spark gap" is too great for it to jump. Metal fittings attached to the interior are effectivly part of it. Some ovens have unattached metal parts inside the cavity, and metal can be used like this providing certain conditions are satisfied. The designers will have considered all relevant factors and made sure that these components are able to do their job without causing problems.

OUTPUT AND INPUT WATTAGES

A microwave oven consumes about twice its output wattage. This may sound like poor efficiency, but compared with most cookers it is very good indeed, and this is proved by the low cost of cooking household quantities of food by microwave. Some of the "lost" input energy is used to run components such as the blower, timer, turntable and lamp, and the rest goes out as waste heat, mainly from the components cooled by the blower.

BAKING PASTRY

You have probably heard someone say how terrible microwave is for baking pies and suchlike. They probably shouldn't have used microwave in the first place. For pastry, it is not a direct alternative to the conventional oven, but you may not be clear as to exactly why that is. For one thing, it does not provide the high temperature which is needed to bring about the typical baking effect, namely, the browning and the chemical changes in the pastry. Another problem is energy distribution, which is affected by the shape of the pie or other item and its make-up of constituents with different absorption rates.

It is possible to "bake" pastry by microwave, providing a special technique is used. You can learn all about that in a book called Microbaking, which Annemarie has written for Stork margarine.

Plain pastry pieces are a different matter. The shape problem can be overcome, and colour may not matter if they are part of a made up dish. Some recipes include a certain amount of pastry, but it is not likely to envelop the other ingredients as it might with a pie.

SERVICING

First we must establish what is meant by servicing. It has been known to mean no more than checking for radio leakage, by passing a meter around the door. That is not servicing, and some local authorities will carry out such a check free of charge. Approved leakage meters are very costly, and a cheap one is likely to be a complete waste of money. Tests have shown such meters to be wildly inaccurate.

Leakage levels are measured in milliwatts (1,000th watt) per square centimeter at a distance of 5 centimeters from the oven. In the U.K., the current permissible level for a used oven is five milliwatts, and for a new oven, one milliwatt. Some manufacturers have much higher factory standards.

A service does include a leakage check, but it also entails dismantling the oven to some degree, depending on the model. Certain parts then have to be cleaned and perhaps adjusted to ensure that they are doing their job properly. This is mainly connected with the door interlock and cooling systems. An engineer with a specialist knowledge of a particular model can sometimes forestall troubles. The mains voltage should always be checked as the oven is given a final test for performance and cool running.

It is debatable whether that test should be of any great accuracy, providing the owner has found nothing wrong with performance. For example, it could cause unnecessary concern if an engineer pointed out that a 650 watt oven is producing only 595 watts. That does not necessarily show that the oven is faulty. It could have been like that all along, and well within specification tolerances, which might be plus or minus twelve per cent. The actual oven output is one of the normal variables. It would be almost impossible for every specimen of a model to have an output of precisely its rated value - without considerable increases in production costs and selling prices. Microwave output cannot be adjusted by turning screws or anything of that sort.

WHEN IS SERVICING NEEDED?

This depends almost entirely on how much the oven is used, and on its working conditions. There is an airflow through all microwave ovens, and so grease and other pollutants in the atmosphere are its enemies. Where there are animals around the house, especially if they are large dogs, a great deal of dust can build up inside the oven's cooling system. Frying in the vicinity of the oven accelerates the build up of undesirable fat deposits in the cooling system, and on door switch mechanisms, where they may eventually cause a blown fuse.

An oven used only occasionally in a clean atmosphere can remain in perfect condition for several years, but one operating under adverse conditions can be in need of attention annually.

The small print

DOOR SWITCHES

Most microwave oven doors have a number of switches which are actuated, not all at once, as the door is opened. Usually, the last one to operate is designed to put the oven permanently out of action if one of the others has failed. For example, it could place the oven fuse almost directly across the mains supply, which would quickly blow it. This ensures that an engineer is called to deal with the fault. With many models, the first switch is coupled to the door latch (handle or push button) so that it is able to switch off the microwave energy before the door begins to open.

OVEN DOORS

There are many misunderstandings about what keeps the microwaves inside the oven, and stops them coming out around the door. Microwave door seals are nothing like other types of seal and they do not have to be airtight, watertight or even a close fit. For example, steam coming out around the door does not indicate that there is anything wrong with the microwave seals. Air from the cooling system is usually forced into the oven cavity, and so it is under pressure to find its way out again. Not all of it will necessarily pass out through the vents and some may quite normally find its way out around the door. Nowadays, the main area of the door is usually of glass or plastics, inside and out, but those materials do not themselves keep in the microwave energy. The real barrier is sandwiched somewhere in the middle, and is made of metal, either woven wire or perforated sheet. Such materials can appear almost transparent as part of the door. Before being assembled into the door, they look and feel remarkably dense.

In the old days, microwave oven doors had nothing more than perforated metal across them. Air and steam poured straight out through the door, and extra vents were quite unnecessary. The doors were rather difficult to clean and there was always the possibility that something could be pushed through the "mesh". There was once a Norfolk publican who's silhouette was spattered on the wall behind him. An egg in its shell had exploded and gone through the door screen of his microwave oven. His daughter knew no better than to try to reheat a hard boiled egg that way. The modern inner and outer coverings protect the real microwave barrier against damage, and make the doors easy to clean and more pleasing in appearance.

One reason for a microwave door not closing too tightly, is that it usually has a latch which has to apply upward or downward pressure to operate a switch. If the door is held closed by the hook of such a latch, and if that is abnormally tight, the switch might sometimes not work, and likewise the oven. Very old microwave oven doors did have to fit tightly. Relatively few of that type were ever sold to the British public, and since the late seventies, leading makers have fitted three types of seal on every door. This type of door has a frame with quite a solid inner surface, whereas the old type had a wide rim of thin springy metal which had to close tightly enough to grip a cigarette paper all round.

Do remember that no one has ever been found to have been harmed by energy from a microwave oven. That includes the old and now extinct ovens, some of which had high power and very poor doors by present day standards. One old oven was so powerful that it could heat an individual meat pie in just seven seconds, Door interlock switches make it impossible to operate the oven unless the door is firmly closed, and with most models, latched. These switches are quite critically set, and if they get out of adjustment, the oven will either work intermittently or not at all. That shows that they are capable of doing their job, and that they would provide protection if the door became distorted. Only a qualified engineer should ever be permitted to disturb the adjustment of a microwave oven door.

POST SCRIPT

Non-intermittent variable power was introduced just as this book went to the printers. Although this welcome development is not likely to effect much microwave work, it will give an accurate energy level even for short periods, and will help delicate foods which bob up and down with a pulsed system.

What went wrong

RE-HEATING
Baked beans or Brussels sprouts jumping off plate.
    Heated too long, or not grouped together well enough.
Pies soggy.
    Cover used, or overheated by judging pastry temperature instead of filling, or pastry too flaky for good results.
Parts of plated meal underheated.
    Food uneven in height, or dissimilar starting temperatures.
Cold in centre of large amounts, e.g. lasagne, shepherds pie.
    Unsuitable container, or heated continuously. Several progressively shorter spells give better results.

MEAT
Beef joints not browning.
    Cooked too fast, see meat section.
Meat tough.
    Cooked too fast, unsufficient standing time, unsuitable cut for microwave cooking, or poor butcher.
Casserole meat chewy.
    Cooked too fast. Use the advice given in main text.
Joint not cooked as required.
    Thermometer in wrong place, or insufficient standing.

POULTRY
Raw around the bones.
    Not de-frosted properly. Not cooked long enough.
Excessive shrinkage of flesh on portions.
    Overcooked.
Meat tough
    Unsufficient standing time.

FISH
Flesh spitting and tails dry.
    Arranged incorrectly, or overcooked.
Skin dry and tough.
    Should have been brushed with fat before cooking.
Fillets cooking unevenly.
    Arranged incorrectly.
Dry eating.
    No cover, insufficient liquid, or overcooked.

VEGETABLES
Potatoes difficult to mash.
>Insufficient water.

Runner beans will not cook.
>Too old.

Cauliflower, or cabbage leaves dehydrated in places.
>Not wetted sufficiently.

Brussels sprouts or potatoes shrunken and hard.
>Overcooked.

Broccoli unevenly cooked.
>Incorrectly arranged in dish.

PUDDINGS
Sponge pudding raw at the bottom.
>Jam was cooked with it, or it had no rack under basin.

Pastry has burned patches.
>Fat rubbed in unevenly, or just overcooked.

FRUIT
Unevenly cooked.
>Irregular ripeness, or sizes. Stirring neglected.

CAKES
Not cooked at base.
>Cooked without a rack.

Has risen and fallen during cooking.
>Overmixed, or oven door opened too long during early stage.

Cake hard.
>Overcooked.

Cake has burned patches.
>Sugar or fat badly mixed.

Biscuits burned in centre.
>Overcooked.

CHRISTMAS FOODS
Refer to special advice given on page 39.